FULL SEND

THE LIFE OF GRIEF

by
Bryce's Mama
- Katherine
Breckenridge

Full Send – The Life of Grief
Copyright © 2025 Katherine Breckenridge

A portion of the sale of every book will be given to THE BRECKENRIDGE NOMADICS PROJECT, a nonprofit established in Bryce's honor and dedicated to helping others live a FULL SEND lifestyle through the fostering of the national amateur sport of mountain biking.

ISBN Paperback: 979-8-9909566-5-0
ISBN E-book: 979-8-9909566-6-7
Publisher: BRECKENRIDGE NOMADICS, LLC
Edited by: J. Stewart Dixon, bookdoneforyou.com

Heartfelt Acknowledgements

Walking alongside a grieving mama is challenging on so many levels – and, it is not complete on "day one." It lasts day in and day out – for a lifetime.

Thank you to the following who "showed up" and continue to help hold me together – who let me say Bryce's name – again and again and again:

Clare, Sallie, Dad (Dick), Mom (Clare), Alison, Faith, Karen, Farrah, Susie, Steve, Claudia, Paul, June, Patty, Edgar, Richard, Amy, Sandra, CJ, Jenny, Micky, Amanda, Sarah, Daniel, Angie, Malinda and Tim, Steve S., Jennifer, Tim, and David.

You held space for me when I could not show up for myself, when I did not have the energy/focus/wherewithal to return a phone call, text, or answer my front door – when retreating behind my fence was safety/when isolation was solace . . . and, still you have not given up.

Thank you to Cody, Maddie, Kolten, Courtney, Baylor, Jenna, Jake, Luke, Knox, Kim, Laura, and McKenna who love Bryce in a most beautiful way, and have "stood in the gap" in extraordinary ways - who are now family to me.

With love,

Katherine

Table of Contents

In Honor of

Every word, every expression in the following pages is written in honor of my precious son, Bryce Ray Breckenridge. His spirit is the same in death as it was in life – truly a guiding force and example of living life FULL SEND, leaving nothing on the trail.

Dedicated to

The love poured into writing this book is dedicated to my beautiful children, Clare and Bryce. We may be a small family unit, but we stick together – even in spirit.

Introduction

*Grief . . . mere survival and
hope may not be elusive.*

Why this book? Isn't grief hard enough that one doesn't have to dwell on it more by reading a book? Wouldn't it be better to just stuff those feelings down, and then stuff them down again?

Grief doesn't work like that. Oh, you can try to box those feelings, but that containment is temporary, and when grief does present itself, when it escapes from that box, the emotions are ones for which we are completely unprepared.

For me, writing this book has meant facing a multitude of complexities. When few books provided answers – there were no roadmaps, no guidebooks . . . of course there weren't, because grief is very personal . . . I put pen to paper to capture my journey. The course of the writing, which captures events, feelings, poems, and steps taken, has been therapeutic and a means of celebrating my precious son, Bryce.

I make no apology for what you will read in the ensuing pages. You will see grief at its rawest, despair at its deepest, anger with no place to put it, a struggle to hold on – with questions of to what and why, swear words and praises, as well as glimpses of happiness.

I ask that if you feel you have the right to sit in judgment, then put this book down now; it is not meant for you.

Even though there are no definitive answers to grief in this or any book, perhaps within the pages of this writing you will find a pathway to keep going . . . that mere survival and hope may not be elusive.

A World Without Oxygen

*Grief – the kind experienced when
losing a child, is a time with which I
am not sure I can be trusted.*

Grief. It is unwelcome, uninvited – a rawness that invades and permeates everything. At the onset, I thought of grief as a monster – now, I am cautious to use that word as I am learning and experiencing if I did not love Bryce in the consuming/complete/unconditional way a mama does, then the grief would be fleeting – it is here to stay.

My world, as I knew it, was turned upside down in one moment. My son, Bryce, my best friend/my person/my joy, was taken from this earth just as he was reaching a beautiful cadence in life.

I so wish Bryce had outlived me. The bottom line is, I do not think I can live another day without him. That is the truth. That is pain. That is grief. That is depression. That is – *having no oxygen at all.* That is having one's world shift in such a way that nothing makes sense – nothing is recognizable. I look for Bryce everywhere and in everything – around every corner – in every moment.

The pain is so horrible that to this day, months after the accident, I still scream without warning. Today's anguish was raw – "How could You take him when I wasn't with him?" I was Bryce's protector. I was his person. Bryce was my person. How could something so tragic occur, and I was not there – was not by his side – did not even get to say a "goodbye?"

1

As most parents think of their children, in this mama's eyes, Bryce was perfect. Being Bryce's mama is my greatest joy.

This journey of trying to "go on," to get oxygen, to continue living, is excruciating and isolating. There is nothing that compares to what is required of one as each moment is faced. The loss of a child, the grief that ensues – it changes everything. Who you are now is different than who you were when your child was on this earth. You know something that others do not: that nothing matters except seeing your child again. The constant thinking about your child is all-consuming – how to get to your child, how long it will be until you see your child again, will you see your child again . . . those thoughts dominate.

You will go through the motions of getting dressed, working, putting a smile on your face because it is the polite thing to do . . . no one wants to (needs to or will) understand your grief, shrieks of grief, and your grief bursts. You will feel alone. People who you thought would stand by you become strangers; others who you may not have known well become your support system. Your world will appear to be spinning out of control, nothing may make sense, and you may operate in a fog for some time, if not for all of time.

Bryce and I had been through some very challenging life events, and I thought God could trust me with the hard times. Grief – the kind experienced when losing a child – is a time with which I am not sure I can be trusted. Every day I somehow manage to get out of bed while feeling the weight of fatigue, extreme body aches, deep sorrow, and despair, and I try to do something – anything positive that may be considered a forward motion.

What I do know is as my search for Bryce continues – every day, I scream, "Bring him back."

During a recent time when I was sharing my anguish with my daughter, Clare, her words of wisdom still resonate with me. "Mom, you and Bryce shared a bond that was so unique and special. It is a love that no one else will know or understand.

You won't be able to duplicate that, but you can continue to carry that with you."

I am trying to make my way through this nightmare. I share elements of this early journey with you, hoping that grief is something you can move with rather than get buried under and that you, too, will be able to carry with you the treasured relationship you had with your child.

Searching for Bryce

I may smile – that is a mask.

This morning, as I took a picture of the sky from my kitchen window, I saw the blue the color of Bryce's eyes. I turned and looked into his eyes, looking into the camera when a treasured picture was taken, and wept deeply as I longed to hold my precious child.

Moments later, I came across a reel on social media – it was as if Bryce was speaking to me. "Do not mourn me, don't drown me in black cloth and quiet whispers. Laugh loud, drink deep, tell the stories that made me live. Remember the bad jokes, the nights that stretched into dawn, the times we swore we'd never forget . . . and don't. I was here, a life well lived. I want something more than tears. So raise a glass and dance a little. Let the wind take my name . . . I'll be listening. Do not mourn me, celebrate me." – The Wandering Paddy.

And then I heard the wind chimes.

The raw truth . . .
What is life
without my son?
I wish I had died
that day, too. I
may smile – that
is a mask, it is
momentary – it
is just to be
polite.

Perhaps
momentary
happiness and
then reality is oh,
so present. The
smile is to make
you feel more
comfortable. I
want to rip out
my heart. The
pain is too big.

Life No Longer

The "before" and then the "after."

Photographs – there are those that signify the "before" and those that signify the "after." The "before" – when life had hope – when I knew I would hear my son's voice, when I made his dinner, could listen to his dreams

. . . the "after" – that smile . . . fleeting, if one looked closely, that deep sorrow in my eyes.

Boulders, and Streams, and Jumps! Oh, Yes!!!

An Estate Planning Article
Highlighting Bryce – Written when
he was about sixteen years old.
Write as many incredible chapters
as you can throughout life.
By: Katherine S. Breckenridge

Parking Straight Ahead! How many times have you seen a road sign, felt the anticipation of finally ending up at your destination spot, and then once you've arrived, wished you could recapture the journey? Or, maybe even scripted the chapters differently?

A few weeks ago, I found myself deep in the woods, moving at what felt like breakneck speed, with ravines to the left, a tight

turn approaching on the right, and a fallen tree straight across the narrow, dirt path. The scenario did not seem ideal for one who likes to remain in control, to plan for the foreseeable and the unforeseeable possibilities, and to guard against risk and liabilities.

I was thankful, breathed an audible sigh of relief, and had a quick and very descriptive conversation with nobody but the trees (makes one wonder what is heard in the forest when no one is listening), when the signpost on the bike path read, "PARKING," and the arrow gave the directional to the closest parking lot. My instinct was, "get me there, and fast!"

"Wait a minute; not so fast," I cautioned myself, as I held on tight to the handlebars of my mountain bike and tried to maneuver down the steep, rocky grade of the bike path. Though my son was now nowhere in sight, as one of the bikers on the trail described, my "flying son" was now yards upon yards ahead of me. After waiting patiently for me to catch up, and just moments before my son took off (again) in a spurt of energy, he had been sharing his story with me.

I realized at that moment, no longer was I the storyteller of L. Frank Baum's, The Wizard of Oz's, "Lions, and tigers, and bears! Oh, my!" My son was now the storyteller. His version was, "Boulders, and streams, and jumps! Oh, yes!!!" Awesome parenting moment!

The realization that my son was sharing a part of his world with me, made me wish I could stop time. Precious time. How had time advanced so quickly that my story chapters were somewhat dimmed, and his were rising to the forefront?

As a parent, we celebrate when our children grasp the tools to develop and tell of their own productive and exciting adventures. And, hallelujah, when they choose to share some of their storylines with us!

Though the chapters of our lives may ebb and flow based upon our age, the needs of our family, our careers, our bucket list choices, and the audiences, the importance of what we share at two pinnacles of our lives seems to have an eternal effect; so, write wisely.

The first is what we tell others by our actions and words. That thought reminds me of the lyrics in a song by Sara Groves, *Tent in the Center of Town*, "There's a tent in the center of town and the people are losing their frowns cause they think they'll go

there and see lions and bears in the tent in the center of town…
There's a tent in the center of town where the people can gather
around who wouldn't step foot in a church but who aren't afraid
of a good news crusade in the tent in the center of town."

I pray that as we reach out to others, our actions and words are
not hindered, and that they tell the story of the good news
crusade, helping to build a welcome to those in our community
who are at various levels of preparation. So many need a
listening ear, someone to come alongside them as they adapt to
changing expectations, and someone to understand how special
they are – that they have something to contribute to our
community.

Second, what one leaves in writing for interpretation at the end
of one's life, often has the opportunity to tell a final story. As
an estate planning attorney, I see so many variations of Wills
and Trusts, each reflective of what has transpired during the
Testator's or Grantor's life. Often, family relations are
harmonious, giving joy to the Testator or Grantor in the writing
of a Will and/or Trust. There are times when relations may be
acrimonious, and the drafting reflects those situations.

I encourage others to memorialize their intentions for their
assets. If one does not, they may not be able to script their estate
story the way they intend, and their assets will be distributed as
set forth by the Commonwealth.

If you are anticipating a "perfect ending" as you see it, and
controlled by you, whether that means you have wonderful
family relationships, strained family relationships, or no
relationships at all, I encourage you to plan ahead; write as many
incredible chapters as you can throughout life, and prepare for a
last chapter that is reflective of your story; perhaps considering
it a sequel at arms-length.

The Descent of Grief

Raw Grief – The Day the World Changed

"This is [unidentifiable name] *from* [rescue/EMT] *we did all we could for your son; unfortunately, he did not make it."*

The message had to be received by someone else. The deafening shrieking could not have been coming from me. The immediate knowledge that something horribly wrong – devastatingly permanent – had occurred, something so personal, so out-of-my-control. The shrieking continued. I was going to throw up – my body lost control. I could not find shelter – a dark, alone space fast enough; somewhere to bury my head, to stop this reality – the immediate pain. This. Could. Not. Be. Happening.

Just moments ago, I had been in Lowe's when the first call came from Cody. "Bryce has been in an accident. The medevac is on its way. My grandparents are going to the end of the road to meet the ambulance. Bryce hit his head pretty hard. Bryce is unconscious, but he is breathing. He is strong. He is a fighter." In addition to me stating, "Let me know what hospital to head towards." Somewhere in my broken sentences were fragments of, "Oh, my . . . Tomorrow, is his birthday . . . This can't be happening . . . How do I get to Bryce . . . Where will they take Bryce . . . Oh, God, please."

During the rush to get home . . . Call my daughter. "Meet me at home. Bryce is being medevacked." Call my sister. "Please pray. Bryce has been in a motocross accident, and a medevac is on its way."

Moments later, as I made a few frantic calls requesting prayer coverage for Bryce, I was throwing items into an overnight bag, and my daughter was telling me to breathe.

Then the call – that stranger's voice informing me of the worst news a mother could ever receive. He must have been mistaken. This happens to others, not to my son. My son, who just that morning had told me, "Riding on that track is exactly what I had wanted to do today. I am excited."

The birthday plans were in place. The presents waiting to be presented. How could the hug, shared just the day before, have been the last of such an occurrence? How could we have known that the phone calls on that Friday – our daily two or three, and then the phone call Saturday morning – would now echo in the halls of my memory. The precious exchanges of, "I love you. Love you. Love you," were truly so priceless.

I wonder, as I look back, were any of the exchanges and thoughts a foreshadowing of what was to come?

Bryce handed me a gift card he hadn't used and said, "If nothing else, it will be Christmas." Just a week before the accident, when I hugged Bryce, I listened closely to his heart beating. During that same time period, Bryce painted a mountain scene on slate and said, "This is for you, Mama – you keep it."

Bryce always told the dogs, "I'll be back." This time, Lincoln was growling a lot – as if he knew and did not want Bryce to leave.

Before he left the house for the last time, Bryce and I stood for more than half an hour at the front door, not rushing, just talking about aspects of the car he drove and his next off-roading adventure. As Bryce was walking towards his car, I took photos of him.

Day One

Tell her to stop talking.

Even on "day one," there were decisions, logistics – ones with which a mother should never be faced. Calls to the funeral home – "We have already sent someone to transport your son back to Virginia." "Do you want to meet tomorrow or on Monday? You won't be able to see Bryce tomorrow because of the nature of the accident." Me, "Tell her to stop talking." Until that point, I did not know many details. That image plagued me night after night – How could my precious, perfectly created son be so hurt? I found myself grabbing my neck, and jaw – believing, if I think this through enough, I can reverse it. I even searched for medical and scientific reasoning that Bryce could have survived such a horrific accident. The "but for" kept running through my mind . . .

Day Two

Somehow, I must reverse time so that I can fix this.

Day two. That awful "next day" when the sun rises, the world still goes about its business, and there I was – left in a fog of trying to decipher if I was in a nightmare. This could not be happening. Surely, Bryce would be walking through the front door at any moment, or calling me as he got close to home to ask me to let him in the side gate. How do I stop the shrieking? How do I breathe? Somehow, I must reverse time so that I can fix this. Bryce had been on this earth just twenty-four hours ago. I am Bryce's mom; surely, I can change the course of time, of events. My heart was shattered. That Sunday felt like an eternity – excruciatingly painful, yet surreal. At nine-thirty that morning, Bryce would have turned twenty-seven. The day was cold, rainy . . . I wrote a letter to Bryce, placed it in his birthday card, and watched as the flames and wind took it, burning it in the firepit – hoping Bryce would know the words of love enclosed.

The Prelude – A Beautiful Life of Adventure

The Obituary

**Bryce loved to find a mountain top
to watch the sunset.**

Writing Bryce's obituary – I had planned it in my head during the night hours and tried to capture the vibrancy of his spirit.

"Death can be so inconvenient. You try to live and love. It comes and interrupts . . . She still had things to say . . ." from Sara Groves' "What Do I Know." We still had things to say to precious Bryce – Bryce Ray Breckenridge, born on the third day of December, 1996 – and ushered to Heaven on the wings of angels as he was doing what he loved doing, riding motocross with some of his best friends, on the second day of December, 2023, the day before his twenty-seventh birthday.

Bryce loved the Lord in a quiet, beautiful, confident way, and his favorite book of the Bible was Revelation. "Here I am! I stand at the door and knock. If anyone hears my voice and opens the door, I will come in and eat with that person, and they with me. To him who overcomes, I will give the right to sit with me on my throne, just as I overcame and sat down with my Father on His throne." Revelation 3:20-22 NIV

Those who knew Bryce witnessed his love of life and his means of celebrating through the adventure sports of mountain biking, motocross, snowboarding, backcountry overlanding and mountaineering, water skiing, wakeboarding,

paddleboarding, split-boarding, sailing, surfing, and wood-working/building.

For Bryce, the perfect beginning to a day of enjoying the outdoors was to rise early to catch the sunrise. Following a day of work, Bryce loved to find a mountain top to watch the sunset while enjoying a fire, often Facetiming so his mother could bear witness, before descending the mountain top in search of pizza.

Bryce loved his name and claimed the following Bible verse, "Fear not, for I have redeemed you; I have called you by name; you are mine. When you pass through the waters, I will be with you; and when you pass through the rivers, they will not sweep over you." Isaiah 43:1-2 NIV

Bryce's family finds comfort in the winter season, envisioning him looking down from the biggest mountain top, with just the right amount of snow, as he begins his descent on his snowboard, cheered on by Jesus. Knowing he had the perfect run, and that the next day – or in Heaven's time, the next adventure – Bryce will likely be paddleboarding around Heaven's replica of Canandaigua Lake. We that remain on this earth will continue to serve where we can and will celebrate that Bryce is now living the best life!

Bryce was a very private person and never wanted to be the center of attention; respecting this, the burial service will be private, with plans for a celebration of Bryce's life to be shared as the family comes to terms with this huge loss of life, joy, and beauty.

A Private Service

The service reflected Bryce's pure faith.

The graveside service, that freezing day of December 6th, was private with about twenty-five people present. Surrounding Bryce were the people he loved the most, including his core group of friends; these mountain men stood behind me in a unified presence. I had selected a casket called "Tacoma" because it was the closest to a Toyota brand available. Facing down on the casket was a twelve-foot orange "Maxxis" banner – one of Bryce's favorite mountain bike tires.

Facing up was a six-foot Rocky Mountain banner – Bryce's absolute favorite bike brand.

On the side of the casket, I taped a sticker from Splinters – Bryce's favorite board shop in Vermont.

Bryce worshipped God in the mountains – he did not worship within the four walls of bricks-and-mortar, but found God's Spirit in His Creation. The service reflected Bryce's pure faith.

Surrounded by those Bryce loved the most, Bryce's faith and his love of the outdoors and adventure sports were shared. Then, each of Bryce's core group taped their race jerseys, goggles, gloves, and lift passes to the top of the casket – Bryce was truly a celebrity. On top of the race jerseys, white roses were taped by each person present. It was a service unlike any other. If a service had to happen, it was just what Bryce would have wanted.

A Celebration – Bryce's Style

Following the graveside service, people from near and far made their way to Reddish Knob – one of the highest points in Virginia, and one of Bryce's treasured spots.

It had snowed, and the trek was icy – perfect Bryce weather. There was a long line of cars that wound their way up that mountain.

Watching the sun set and the evening shades turn the mountain views into sights of lights twinkling in the far distant valley, we gathered around a campfire, ate pizza – Bryce's style, and recounted stories about Bryce.

One after another shared about Bryce –

- An avid outdoorsman.
- His fearlessness.
- His kindness.
- His giving.
- His expertise.
- The way he encouraged others.

- How he often hung at the back of the pack when mountain biking, so he could cheer on the rest, even though his skill exceeded those present.
- That he never had to be the center of attention.
- How others strove to be like him.
- The quiet steadfastness of his faith.
- How he lived his life full send.
- The beauty of both his spirit and his presence.

A Visual of Grief

A quiet dignity.

My son's body lies within the earth beside me. This beautiful man, who carried himself with a quiet dignity – who rode bikes like the wind, is now stationary.

Space Redefined

A place that was set aside
for just Bryce and me.

Before Bryce's accident, I loved my dining room – the antiques, the stories, and the meaning they held.

All that changed on that horrible day. Though Bryce's spirit is best felt outside in the mountains, I needed a quiet, dedicated space within our home. As life shifted, my dining room became overrated and the antiques – now, no longer important. I got rid of my dining room furniture and created a place that was set aside for just Bryce and me – a place removed from the world where I journal messages to Bryce, talk with Bryce, play music with Bryce . . . The china cabinet – removed:

In its place is Bryce's bike – hung on the wall with a Bike Stop sign (Bryce's first job) behind it, and a light shining onto the bike. The bike, which once carried Bryce as he flew down the mountain trails and over technical jumps reserved for the few, is now stationary for the rest of time and is what I stand near and hug and can feel Bryce's spirit.

Priceless.

Christmas

The Breckenridge Star

Christmas was a blur – just three weeks after Bryce's accident . . . no joy could be found.

I placed a Christmas tree in Bryce's room, and on it I hung his favorite ornaments. The gifts that were exchanged – each was significant of Bryce . . . something to do with the mountains, his love of mountain biking, or his faith.

Clare watched me struggle in my search for Bryce – night after night. In answer to that, she presented me with the coordinates of a star that is now forever named after Bryce. So, when I look to the Heavens, I can find the star.

Sunday, December 31ˢᵗ, 2023

I have called you by name.

My Precious Bryce – Here we are on the last day of 2023 – with your passing, it is now the worst year EVER. Rationally, I should be welcoming in 2024; I am not, as I want to hold on to 2023 for as long as possible, since 2023 is the last year on earth that you knew.

I CANNOT stand being separated from you. You are my life – my joy – my reason for being. You were everything beautiful to me. I loved your adventurous spirit – how you loved nature – how your mind worked – how you celebrated life in a way that was different from me, and I learned from you how to appreciate the things of nature – the outdoors – the sunrises and sunsets.

Time itself is so very, very painful. If/when I sleep, I wake up in disbelief and have to process that this nightmare is not going away. I cannot believe that part of my vocabulary now is "obituary," "gravesite," "passing away," and language that uses the past tense.

I sing to you at the gravesite – I tell you about what your friends and I may be doing. I plead with God. I play music for you. I WEEP and WEEP. I read Bible verses. Life is surreal. Life is horrible. There is no point to it right now.

I want to yell and scream at God . . . and, I do. It is not pretty. I always thought of God as kind . . . this is the absolute cruelest thing I could have ever (NEVER) imagined.

When I visited you at your gravesite today – as I do every day – I read Isaiah 43: 1-2 to you. I began to dissect the Bible verse:

(1) Fear not – Is that for you or for me? Am I to no longer be afraid? Do you have what you need? Are you warm? Fed? Cared for? Loved? Are you happy? Do you know I love you? Will I see you again? WILL I SEE YOU AGAIN?!!! How long do I have to wait to see you?

(2) For I have redeemed you – Should I draw comfort from that? Is that a guarantee that you are okay? Again and again, I have prayed that since God did not answer my Lazarus Prayer (it's been three days – PLEASE bring Bryce back), and He did not answer my Christmas Prayer (PLEASE bring Bryce back – let this be a Christmas miracle), and He did not answer my Modern-Day Miracle Prayer (PLEASE bring Bryce back – let Bryce be a modern-day miracle) . . . that he would either resurrect you OR that the Rapture would occur.

I begged God to let me be with you – I DO NOT WANT TO BE ON THIS EARTH WITHOUT YOU. You and I always told each other that we could not live on this earth without the other. WHY am I still here?

Also, I process the imagery in my mind all of the time – I cannot get beyond that you may have been hurting and that I was not physically present for you. I watch the times of day as the hours of a Friday turn to Saturday . . . I remember each horrifying moment. I WANT YOU HERE WITH ME, or I WANT TO BE WHERE YOU ARE. IS there "a place" where you are? I trusted that there was a hedge of protection over you . . . and, then this . . . What can I therefore trust? You were the most beautiful human being God created – this world is definitely not a better place without you here. I do not know how to keep going.

(3) I have called you by name. That means that God knows you – knows me. He knew if He had your name written in the Book of Life, and that December 2nd at

1:44 PM, you would be in such a horrific accident and then would be pronounced gone from this life at 2:19 PM – that I could not live without you. He knows my name, too. WHY THIS TRIAL?!?!!!!???? I. Am. Not. Okay.

(4) You are mine. Okay – it was that part that really got to me earlier today when I was visiting you at your gravesite.

I drew strength from my "foundational faith," telling myself that God had given you to me as a gift for the twenty-seven years we shared, and that if *He* wanted you back, who was I to question such a decision?

I will share – I am questioning everything right now. If I believed ALL, then WHY this? HOW this? My very being has been ripped apart. YOU were my life – my precious son! There is no reason to keep going. You were beauty to me.

If I push back too hard, and fail in my "foundational faith," it means that there is no forever – no ever seeing you again . . . I feel that I have to keep asking – keep searching – for both of us. I have to somehow find my way back to the Truth – to try to trust, or all will be for naught.

I ask that if there is any way you can surround me – walk with me throughout each day until I get to you, please, please do so. I so want to know you are here with me.

As 2023 is ushered out by 2024, I don't know what to expect, how to make it through time at all, or what "purpose" itself even looks like . . . I love you more than life itself.

I look for you everywhere. You are my best friend. I love you – you are my person.

Each night, in answer to your nightly question, my answers have changed – "Everything is locked up. The dogs are okay. I. AM. NOT. OKAY."

You promised, "I'll be back." I am counting on that.

My precious, precious son – Bryce, I love you.

A Letter to a Few

When others reached out . . .

I am sharing the following with just a few people who mean so much to me – please keep it close to your heart.

Bryce was my joy/my life. There are no words to describe what this pain is like. My beautiful, precious, perfectly made son – taken so early in life in a horrific accident . . . As the grief infuses every part of my being, my mind and heart search for answers.

I am so very thankful for the prayer coverage, kind gestures, and notes of encouragement that so many have shared. Though I have not had the strength/focus to respond, each has been treasured and has helped me for a moment to "reset" my mind/spirit.

A mama's pain . . . At day three of this awful journey, I prayed (pleaded/begged) what I call "the Lazarus Prayer," begging God to bring Bryce back to me. Then I prayed the "Christmas Prayer," again begging God to bring Bryce back to me. Then I prayed for a "Modern Day Miracle;" please God, bring Bryce back to me. I now pray for Resurrection or for the Rapture.

I love being Bryce's mama, and now I am not sure what life is supposed to look like. I am struggling to find a footing, and in this, I am holding on to every memory – Bryce's friends have shared with me so many thoughts and memories, all of which I will treasure deep in my heart. In addition to how Bryce impacted his friends by sharing his faith during many deep, meaningful conversations – truly changing the course of their lives – it is the legacy of kindness and talent he leaves with those he knew.

Bryce lived life to its fullest – through his adventure sports and his love of the outdoors. The following are just a few of the thoughts sent by Bryce's friends; I hope you will find comfort and inspiration in them, as I do.

"I just want you to be aware of the impact Bryce had on so-so-so many people and everyone who knew him has the best things to say. He might have left this world, but he was a celebrity in the biking world and those who knew him will forever remember him for who he was and his impeccable talent."

"Bryce has truly left a piece of himself in every person he interacted with. The love and care for him by everyone he encountered is immeasurable and truly inspiring. And for this his life was a true success in the eyes of God."

"If we could all manage to live each day a little more like Bryce, the world would be a much brighter more beautiful place."

Time itself is painful. Thank you for walking alongside Bryce's sister, Clare, and I as we navigate our way through this. We claim the following:

We'll Meet Again On The Mountain
In Memory of Bryce Ray Breckenridge
&
His Full Send Spirit

Sister's Wedding

Bryce's spirit was present.

Bryce had RSVP'd to my sister, Sallie's, wedding, which was held a month after the accident.

Packing an overnight bag, getting into the car, going on a journey that Bryce had planned on being on, carrying an indescribable pain, yet wanting to celebrate my precious sister – it was like trying to wrestle two opposite emotions within one heart – a heart that was completely shattered.

Bryce loved Sallie and her family, and he would have wanted us to attend. As Clare and I made the eight-hour journey to South Carolina, my precious daughter continued to be the rock. I was still in shock, in disbelief, and she let me talk about Bryce non-stop.

The waterfront wedding was the most beautiful I have ever seen, and Sallie was the most stunning bride – full of grace and elegance. Bryce's spirit was present in that very chair set between Clare and me: It was adorned with flowers, a miniature sailboat, and his name. I think I may have left an imprint on Clare's hand. I held it so tightly as the tears flowed – so much pain, so much beauty.

Jake's Visit

It was a reflection of Bryce.

Each of Bryce's friends carries a part of Bryce with them. When I interact with them, it feels like I am holding on to a part of Bryce.

Shortly into the new year, Jake, one of Bryce's dear friends, spent the day with me. The afternoon was cold and rainy. He met me in what is now my old office, and I got to show him the new office space I was considering.

Over the years, Bryce and Jake had gone on countless adventures – mountain biking, snowboarding, split-boarding, visiting mountain tops, as well as spending hours upon hours exploring career and life goals.

Those hours Jake and I shared in Bryce's hometown – over lunch, visiting Bryce's gravesite – the tears shed – the gentle hug, and at the house – those were treasured moments – ones during which someone who knew Bryce, and who loved Bryce, allowed me to talk about Bryce as much as I needed to. The time spent was kind, gentle, safe – it was a reflection of Bryce. I will forever hold those moments deep in my heart.

So here's to one badass, kindhearted, passion fueled, God fearing, big sending, outstanding outdoorsman. We love you brother. To Brycycle!

Cheers everybody 🤙🤘

A Poem About Bryce

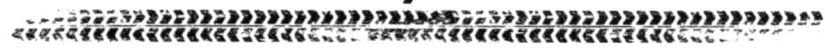

For Bryce Ray Breckenridge
Written with love – Bryce's Mama,
Katherine Breckenridge
Sixth day of February, 2024

A Beauty Indwells – A Full Send Spirit

Unannounced. Uninvited.
    "We did all we could."
Oh, Death, you did just come and interrupt.
Shall I play that drum melody, "Pa rum pum pum pum?"
    The one thing I had that was fit for the King.
    No choice given.
    Nothing withheld.
The Breckenridge Star – though no latitude granted on Earth.
Joy. Adventure. Now deafening silence.
The hedge of protection – a different form.
    No longer a mama's prayer.
That bike. That ramp.
The angel armies grew by one.
    Complete. Irreversible.
A legend in the cycling world – could not envelope you then.
    Grew exponentially as the realms exchanged terms –
    Your quiet, confident faith –
        changing the course for others.
Perfectly and wonderfully made.
    God called you by name – 27 years minus a day.
    Your Full Send spirit obeyed.
Now your car sits idle.
Your cloths neatly folded.
Your bike is stationary.
Perhaps your bucket list redefined.

Oxygen is but a luxury as I search the skies.
Are you the artist behind the sunset?
The shooting star your directional, too?
Grief infused and unbearable.
Recalibration of moments.
Wait, I'm still here?
Why him?
Yes, it was him.
There is no waking from this nightmare.
Time itself is painful.
Exhaustion. Confusion.
The best shot has been taken.
Daily visits to that earthen square; growing grass –
marking the passage of time.
Oh, evil one – you will not win.
I may – Stumble. Scream. Plead. Cry.
But the Holy Spirit dwells within –
and legend will live on.
Beauty in his – Purpose. Vision. Adventure.
All fit for The King.
We'll meet again on the mountain.
And, raise a hallelujah – mountain mug in hand.

A Poem About Removal

People grieve differently, and I respect that. I had just lost my joy, my world, and expressions like "we are family now," are ones that I trusted. The following poem reflects the pain felt when a "friend" of Bryce's decided he could no longer walk alongside my grief.

By: Katherine Breckenridge
March 21, 2024

Removal From the Circle

The silence is deafening.
The balance already unstable.
The foundation in question.
This mama –
     Whose world was her precious son
     Where there was no time for a goodbye
     A phone call reported the transition
The daily communications – now a blank wall
A hand to hold during grace – now an empty chair
No longer a person present
     To play checkers
     To traverse the farm in search of the Christmas tree
     To dream big with
The love of a mama –
     Laundry
     Meals
     Rent
     And, a thing with wheels
Are you sitting at the right hand of Jesus
Do your blue eyes gaze upon Him
Are you warm, cared for, surrounded
Is Heaven really beyond this mama's imagination

How long do I wait?
> The wind, the stars, the sunsets
> Seven, Thirty, or 365

The pain grows
> A despair like none other

Fragile doesn't touch it
> I am all alone
> I am empty
> I am broken
> And, you took a piece of me

Where's my DAMMIT DOLL?!
To know a mama's love and the equivalent grief
This mama clings to the contact of those who love you
Human action becomes oh, so human
To remove oneself from the mama's circle
> A second wave of grief descends
> Cruel
> Selfish
> Untimely
> Unforgiven

My son showed up for you
Now, I am my son
What would Bryce do?
> Certainly not that

A Poem About Grief and Work-Related Vindication

GRIEF UNRELENTING
By: Katherine Breckenridge

A nother day dawns – the ground is still unstable.
    Oh, I'm still here.
    I did not awaken from this nightmare.

There's safety in these sheets and blankets.
    Pulling them back, seemingly futile?
    The dogs need walking.
        There's that.
    Clients are scheduled.
        There is no energy – just a deep fatigue.
    The demands. The world does not understand.
    Time has passed. Time to get going. You should get going.
        No. No. No. It does not work like that.
        You do not know. I hope you never will.

He is my child. Looks. Thoughts. Beliefs.
    His own uniqueness.
        Mountain man.
        Adventurous.
        Full Send.
    I cannot breathe. There is not enough oxygen.

Last night's news – vindication of sorts.
    A firing occurred.
    You saw the truth first –
        the others arrived late to the mountain.
    Too little, too late –
        your dignity stripped – the injustice rendered.
    Remain quiet – true colors are revealed.
    The contrast – you shook hands in the face of lies.

A graveside visit.
>> We went together – your spirit and me.
>> Coffee – a toast to the firing.

Halfway through the day. What did I do this morning?
>> Grief infuses the very crevasses of the mind.
>>> It waits, lurks, pounces – ever present.
>> Still, there are meetings.
>>> Demands of thought. Requirements of knowledge.
>> The black suit and pearls –
>>> a uniform, a shield, perhaps a cape –
>>> reach for it and pieces of the puzzle . . .
>>> there is a fit, if but for a meeting.

There is no soft landing – no space of grace.
>> Perform. Persevere. Disappear. – The choices are few.

A kind message.
>> A lifeline – Bridging one moment to the next.

Evening arrives but not without a price.
>> Work matters persist – the fatigue of grief dominates.
>>> Nothing changed today.
>>> Responsibilities were met, but for what?
>>> Oxygen is still insufficient.
>>> For time spent, what is in its place?
>>> No effort brought him back.

A Poem About Foundations

In March – just a few months after Bryce's accident – I conducted a seminar on estate planning, a commitment made many months before the accident, and thought I could get through the introductory poem – one I like to use to "humanize" estate planning. In the poem I had written to honor my father, I had referenced Bryce water skiing. I lost my composure . . .

A Complexity of Green
By: Katherine S. Breckenridge

His shoulders droop now more than before.
Perhaps from the weight of decision and
    Concern borne by the provider one.
My guess is that the shoulders of this proud,
    Yet humble man, feel the gravity of
A time gone by and a time yet to arrive –
    That time that remains before the threshold.
You see – the knowledge he has is at its height.
He knows that he has provided well for others.
He can find assurance that he supplied his children
    With tools for their toolboxes.
He has been a faithful and loving husband,
    Setting an example where none had been.
For the brick and mortar, his dollars did supply.
The educational credits were his subsidy, too.
The first set of wheels – whether bike or car –
    I am sure a toy he preferred.
The dinner table counsel carried into night to
    Shape the childhood foundations of
    Faith without excuse.

No greater gift could have been given to set us
        On our course.
The walk down the aisle
        Was to know the roots of another generation.
The attendance of little league baseball games and cross
        Country meets is long gone.
The square dancing – a pursuit for those with
        Younger knees.
He has been witness to wars, economic recessions, and
        A merry-go-round of political figureheads.
Like many who hold such vast experience
        And commonsense, could have influenced our
        Great nation if given but a chance.
With slowing movements, a motorboat he may drive –
        Like the pilot I still envision,
        If just to see his grandson fly on water.
The time between now and then – oh, what say you?
Why is this not of dignity? A worry-free composition?
This man who gave all, who planned ahead. Yes, a trust,
        A will, and protective documents . . .
Shall our government be so crass as to tax beyond its
        Seams, so that man may lose his history
        To some complexity of green?
I tell you, the legacy that matters
        He will leave to all intact
        So that we may continue the tradition of
        A compass unfaltering.
This changes not the provider's hard-earned green that he
        Intended for his bride.
With wisdom already imparted, he has paid his fare.
Take back your cruel imbalances of taxing everywhere.
Hands off I say – this is *their* golden years.
We have within our borders the smartest minds I know.
Match them with those who comprehend the challenges
        Of old.
May we, with him, hold our shoulders back when we
        Design a system that guards the threshold with
        A fearlessness – protecting the now to then.

Here's a Book

But for three . . .

Books, books, and more books. There are many books written on grief. My grief is unique to me, and yours is to you.

Out of the approximately twenty books that were given to me within the first four months following Bryce's passing, few were helpful. One book actually stated that one should never, ever get angry at God. WHY NOT? My God is big enough to handle my anger.

Three books helped me during the first few months. Those three are *Bearing the Unbearable* by Dr. Joanne Cacciatorre, *Lament for a Son* by Nicholas Wolterstorff, and *When Bad Things Happen to Good People* by Harold S. Kushner.

Untold Hurtful Comments

Statements – though not intended as cruel, when said to a grieving mama, they cut to the heart.

"At least he was doing what he loved."

"Will you keep his car?"

"Do you have other children?"

"Trust God."

"All in God's timing."

"God is good."

"Count it as joy."

"God has good things in store for you."

"You will get through this."

"Bryce was taken so that his circle of friends would know God."

"Bryce's passing was to send a message to another person; your grief and pain are collateral damage."

"My family and I grieve differently than you. I am removing myself. I have to live my own life."

"Call me if you need anything." (We will never call.)

"The second year is worse." (Why in the world (even if true) would someone share that with a mama who is experiencing grief in the first year and there is no way life seems like it can get worse?")

"Heaven needed another angel."

Unexpected Wisdom

Sharing this precious moment ... This morning was extra hard as I began the selection of a headstone for Bryce's gravesite.

I designed the headstone alone. I sat with the representative from the funeral home to place the order. Then, I left alone – the silence, the feeling of smallness in the vast world, created when undertaking such a surreal action – is life-changing.

Then following some time at the office, I walked towards my vehicle and stopped to talk with a man who is homeless, one with whom I had exchanged brief pleasantries in the past.

I had been tearing up and as he asked how I was doing, I shared about Bryce's passing. He said, "You will always carry his spirit with you." Then, he said, "I have a gift for you."

He reached into his bag which had a Walmart logo on it – I could see empty bottles, etc. He continued to rummage in his bag. Then, he handed me a small piece of wood, painted with praying hands and a Bible verse. He repeated what he had shared. ♥ This gesture was priceless and was...is... so treasured.

A Special Group of People

Bryce was truly a mountain man. Bryce taught me that true beauty is found in nature, and that one must have a balance. As I straddle the worlds of professional work and mountain purity, I am trying to follow in Bryce's footsteps.

Bryce surrounded himself with friends who were like family to him – Cody, Maddie, Baylor, Jenna, Kolten, Jake, and Luke. Each of these individuals is amazing, and their love for Bryce and their way of enveloping Bryce's sister, Clare, and me into their fold has reached into those moments when I did not think I could continue. They understood my son

and have provided strength and continuity to me – a safe place to talk about and to celebrate Bryce.

Meeting on the Mountain

Spending time in the mountains, areas in the outdoors that are uncharted, that celebrate God's creation, is when I feel the closest to Bryce. The sunrises and sunsets – watched on this side of Heaven by Bryce, and now perhaps Bryce has a front row seat and helps design them.

Touching the very stones that Bryce placed on the bike paths at Massanutten. Seeing the dirt jumps and traverses created by Bryce – the ones that help make those mountain bike paths so technical. Sitting with Baylor at the Summit – as we overlooked the valley below, talking about Bryce for hours – the moment was captured in a picture by Jake. Priceless times.

Waterside Reflections

Bringing the SUV that Bryce used to its natural habitat, traversing where only a 4-wheel drive can go, parking, and then hiking to sources of water – favorites of Bryce – in that setting, brings genuine peace and smiles.

"Mama, West Virginia is going to have a freak snowstorm, so Jake and I are going to White Grass tomorrow," Bryce told me that in mid-May of 2023. Though I thought to myself, "A snowstorm in May?" I responded, "Have a great time!" The pictures I saw afterwards bore testament to the eight inches of snow in which my son was able to split-board – he scaled a mountain at White Grass and then snowboarded down.

Following a harrowing sideways slide on a high, icy bridge, and some incredible driving skills of Bryce's friend, Jake, I recently found that mountain, scaled it cross-country ski style, "raised a toast to Bryce at the top," and rode back down. The day was perfect, another eight inches of snow – I believe sent by Bryce, and this mama's heart was full.

The photographs of Bryce compared to the photographs of me –
taken in the same places, approximately nine months apart . . .
there is no question that Bryce is my son – the resemblance is
clear.

Months after that visit to White Grass, I had the opportunity to
introduce Clare to that piece of Heaven – a place so loved by
Bryce. While there, Chip Chase – that person with a beautiful
spirit – helped me select a set of snowshoes. After that visit, I
sent a card and note to Chip that shared the following:

June 9, 2025

Dear Chip:

Good afternoon! I share the following in the hopes that you will
know the very special impact you had on the life of my precious
son, Bryce, and now me.

In May of 2023, my son called me to let me know that the area
around White Grass was going to experience a large snowstorm

51

and that he and his friend, Jake, were going to White Grass to split-board.

Bryce loved White Grass – it was a safe place for him, full of adventure, kind people, and good energy. May of 2023 was the last time Bryce visited White Grass, as he was taken from this earth in a horrific motocross accident on December 2nd, 2023, one day shy of his twenty-seventh birthday.

Jake, Bryce's friend, brought me to White Grass in February of 2024, so that I could cross-country ski. Going to White Grass, was like magic for me. I had not been cross-country skiing for a very long time; in fact, I had not gone on any adventures for a very long time. I am now learning to live through/for Bryce. It snowed that day – about 8 inches. I got to traverse the paths loved by Bryce and celebrate him at the very top. It was during that adventure that I had the opportunity to meet you for the first time. You

were so very kind and took the time, even with so many people around, to let me share about Bryce. You said, "Do this for Bryce." The memories from that day are priceless.

My daughter, Clare, and I visited White Grass near the turn of 2024/2025. You were there that day and sold me a pair of snowshoes that still had "White Grass glitter" on them. The snowshoes were on my bucket list – they will be forever treasured by me because they are from White Grass, and you helped select them for me.

I am writing a book about Bryce and grief – and how to keep living. Attached is an excerpt about White Grass that is part of the draft.

The card accompanying this letter features a picture of Bryce from May 2023 and a picture of me from February 2024 – my counselor designed it for me, and I thought it might bring a smile your way. I am forever grateful for your kindness.

Chip's Beautiful Response

Dearest Katherine,

Wow, what a powerful letter filled with love and appreciation that took us off our feet. THANK YOU for taking the time and effort to send to us, and we are touched to say the least. It must be a burden to have lost Bryce in the prime of his life. So fortunate for us to have met him and to bring some joy in his winter days.

Please come back and see us and we can hug and cry some to make us both feel better in this huge loss. Best Mom and Awesome Son.

Writing a book is a way to express so much love, as well as lost love, that now is ours to share without Bryce. We have lost two grandchildren and can say it's been tough and never seems to go away. We all need each other, especially in times like this.

May the summer bring some inner joy, knowing we have tried our best to bring goodness to the world. Love the fact that you sent such a deep-felt card and note that was received in the same way here. Thank you...forever. With love Chip and Laurie

Connections like the above are what help move me from one moment to the next . . . always seeking Bryce and getting closer to being with him.

All Things in Motion

Bryce was always in motion. That was his forte; he could ride, fix, build, and tell you the ins and outs of things that had wheels or that moved on snow. When Bryce was two years old, he would ride his tricycle to the end of the driveway, get the mail, and ride to the front door saying, "special delivery." Bryce graduated from that tricycle to a bicycle without training wheels when he was three years of age. From there came the skateboards, snowboards, and mountain bikes. Bryce was an avid motocross rider, mountain biker, and snowboarder. His movements were from season to season – as one ended, the next began. It is on my list of goals to begin mountain biking again – in honor of Bryce.

Humor

Bryce had a quick sense of humor, but one had to lean in close enough to hear. One of my favorite jokes that Bryce made was during COVID, when lumber was scarce. Bryce held up a broken, *wooden* skateboard and stated, "Five hundred bucks Mama, 'cause I know what I got." I have tried to memorialize some of Bryce's quick wit in my journaling.

Recently, Bryce had a colonoscopy performed. After the procedure, Bryce was feeling pretty good from the anesthesia. Wanting to thank the physician and being under the influence of the medications, Bryce wanted to shake the physician's hand. The physician would have none of that, so Bryce tried to fist-bump the physician. Again, the physician would have none of that. As the physician left the exam room, Bryce yelled out, "Sorry about the hairy ass!" That was a memorable day, and of course we stopped for pizza on the way home.

Though it has been decades since I have camped, there is no better time than now to spend moments in nature under the stars with Bryce's spirit. When my tent, sleeping bag, cooler, and camping chair arrived, I felt the slightest ray of happiness, which is quite a foreign feeling to me as of late.

When I arrived home from work and Amazon had placed the enormous cooler box right in front of my house, I laughed (feeling like the money spent was worth that smile alone). I laughed even harder when my sister, Sallie, said, "If I lived close to you, I'd put a face on the box and tape T-Rex arms to it!!" Something about having these camping supplies makes me want to make a claim: "My superpower is my camping supplies." Perhaps, I feel that way because I. Did. It. – I am taking on an adventure that is outside of my comfort zone (I like having easy access to a bathroom at night, a guaranteed place to shower in the morning, and a Starbucks nearby), and the camping supplies provide me with a hope of many adventures – all done with Bryce's spirit alongside me.

Gifting

Gift giving has always been my love language, and it was also one of Bryce's love languages. Bryce was an amazing gift giver. I have treasures given to me from Bryce – items like coats, shoes, a hammock, a kayak designed for one with little upper-body strength, and sunglasses. I love each of these items because I know the love that was behind the selection. I want to keep using each, and at the same time, I want to enshrine them so they don't wear out, so they last forever – they are like memory threads to me.

At the time of this writing, I don't feel like I have much to give, but I do know that I have to keep trying – Bryce would want that. Bryce had some very special people in his life. Work has always been my safe place, especially in times of life trials – I have always been able to somehow collect myself, put on my black suit and pearls, and go to the office. Work is what I know. To be near Bryce, I am combining my love for giving *and* for work: I am able to educate Bryce's circle of friends on matters of estate planning, through seminars and consultations.

I am also designing shirts with images and sayings that celebrate Bryce. For now, I present the shirts to Bryce's "core group." These same designs will become part of a company, continued in honor of Bryce.

An Entity

I established an entity that will market clothing that captures Bryce's spirit. This same entity will design and promote accoutrements related to mountain biking and snowboarding. Part of the revenue generated from the sales will provide an avenue of adventure to those who would not otherwise be able to mountain bike or snowboard.

Mother's Day

Mother's Day was especially painful this year. It represents a day when Bryce and I made a crucial decision to change our environment.

Now I was facing the day for the first time without Bryce physically present. Clare, and two of Bryce's friends, Baylor and Jenna, and I went deep into the mountains for the long weekend. We

walked along the bike trails that Bryce had ridden – saw the jump that was made successfully by Bryce and has yet to be made by another. We shared stories, hiked along the water, and watched the sun setting – knowing that Bryce was sharing his firsthand beauty with us.

Precious Clare gifted the following
priceless message to me:

"Mom – There's not a single other Mama C on this earth. Bryce and I have the one and only. I'm not sure how we got so lucky. You show us how to love and be strong – a balance that is so hard for most. Even when faced with adversity, the love you pour out to others does not stop. You have taught and continue to teach us what it looks like to reclaim your life and to not take things lying down. You have faced many things head-on and have used them as building blocks when most would have turned the other direction. Demanding more for yourself and following your dream of law school and not just that but, building a practice for yourself – F'ing Amazing . . . living your life on your terms . . . and now, carrying on a Spirit of Adventure – conquering fears like riding ski lifts/camping/hiking at night and so much more. I know Bryce is getting a kick out of it and smiling that big squinty-eyed smile, laughing a bit as you conquer each of these adventurous things. I love you more than I can put into words – I wish I could count the number of times people tell me how alike we are and it's the best compliment. I am thankful you're my mom. I love you!"

Returning from the weekend was extra challenging – not only because Bryce still had not returned and the house was silent, but on Monday, Clare and I had to say, "good-bye" to our treasured dog, Conrad. Conrad was so loved by Clare, Bryce, and me and had been with us through many trials – that was a hard day. I picture Bryce welcoming Conrad with a huge hug and that beautiful smile!

The group has celebrated many meals at three restaurants in the Harrisonburg Area - Little Italy Pizza at Neff Avenue, Rocktown Kitchen, and Thirsty's. We are creating traditions – they are our "go-to" places for dinner. Bryce's favorite pizza was from Little Italy, and Sandra was like family to Bryce and now to me.

Camping – Whizzbangers Ball

You will always hold a special place in my heart.

I have found that the only time I smile and genuinely mean it right now is when I am over the mountain and amongst Bryce's friends. They love him so much, and they talk about him. I am beginning to live a more balanced life because of Bryce – I am seeking time outdoors and adventuring in a way that is Bryce-inspired.

Each month, I place a "Bryce adventure" in front of me. This month, it was camping. I have not been camping in over forty years, and I have never attended a music festival. This adventure all began with a song. Three Christmases ago, Bryce gifted Tyler Childers' album "Purgatory" to me. It was our Christmas music that year – the year that Bryce and I celebrated Christmas just the two of us – it was one of the best Christmases ever! We moved at our pace – from the morning treasure hunt and opening of stockings, to the decorating of cookies, to the homemade pizza for dinner . . . Every. Single. Moment. was treasured.

Following Bryce's accident, when Bryce's dear friend, Jake, spent a day with me – visiting Bryce's gravesite, sharing stories about Bryce, grieving, and trying to make any sense of the senseless, I shared that Bryce had gifted "Purgatory" to me. A few weeks after the visit, Jake sent me Tyler Childers' three-album set. I put the "Jubilee" record on and felt a moment of joy – and I danced for the first time in a very long time. I felt Bryce – it was his music.

That music was the link to an amazing camping weekend. I found out that Tyler Childers was headlining at Whizzbangers Ball, and four of Bryce's friends, Baylor, Jenna, Jake, Luke and I, bought tickets to the adventure. Planning for the camping trip gave me a ray of hope – something to hold on to.

I purchased items such as a tent, a sleeping bag, a cooler, and a battery pack. With each purchase, I knew that I was getting closer to experiencing Bryce's world.

I prepared treat bags for the journey and a treasure hunt – both were things Bryce loved. I designed "Full Send" shirts for those of us going on the trip.

Having anticipated the camping trip/music festival for months – knowing I would be spending time with people who love Bryce, talk about Bryce, talk and think like Bryce – the weekend could not arrive quickly enough. Yet the day of departure, I awoke feeling anxious, like I had to muster some courage.

Bryce's beloved Land Cruiser was packed in all corners. As I headed over the mountain to meet up with Bryce's friends, I decided to listen to a sermon by Tim Timberlake. Since Bryce's accident, I had not been able to listen to a sermon. I chose this sermon randomly – or so I thought. It was a God thing. The sermon was about miracles and believing God to perform the unimaginable – the miracle that perhaps isn't even rational. The message gave me hope, and at the same time I admit to having the thought "But you haven't been through THIS." So, certainly a miracle, the kind I would like – to have Bryce back on this earth with me – is not what Pastor Timberlake could be referencing. The points made – ones I so wanted to believe for this matter – were ones I filed in my mind to discuss with my grief-trauma counselor.

I arrived at Baylor and Jenna's townhouse. Of course, every good camping trip deserves a Walmart run. God was definitely present in the timing of that day. As we came out of the townhouse, I began walking towards Bryce's vehicle, and I heard a person say, "Who is that woman? Do you know her?" Baylor responded that I am Bryce's mother. The person making the inquiry was Bryce's dear friend from high school, and they had kept in touch – golfing buddies. He had been in Paris when he received the news of Bryce's accident. The reconnection was priceless – a connection on so many levels/so many memories.

Following the Walmart run, we gathered for dinner at Rocktown Kitchen – it was the "core group" – Baylor, Jenna, Cody, Maddie, Ryker, Luke, Jake, and myself.

We then met back at the townhouse, where Kolten joined us as we loaded Bryce's vehicle and Jake's pickup truck with everything except the perishable items.

I stayed the night at a hotel – I was so excited that I could not sleep. We committed to meeting at 8:00 AM. Another God moment. All but Luke and I were running late. It gave Luke and me a few minutes to share some things that had been on our hearts – about Luke losing his father and about his "seeing" me in my grief and the response of a former friend of Bryce's who chose not to walk alongside me, and seemingly the group, in this grief.

Before departing, I gave Baylor, Jenna, Jake, and Luke the treat bags, which, in addition to the travel bingo boards, I had placed some of Bryce's favorite candy – strawberry licorice, Necco wafers, SweeTarts, caramels, Cow Tales, and Carmex lip balm. They received it with the same delight that Bryce would express. My heart was full.

Before making the drive, we grabbed coffee and breakfast at Starbucks – sitting outside with magic in a cup was the perfect send-off. Driving to Whizzbangers in West Virginia was The. Best. Drive. It was like we were teenagers again – going on an adventure and all loving Bryce. We put our phone calls on speaker and played Willie Nelson's "On the Road Again" and Tyler Childers' "Feathered Indians" – favorites of Bryce, and celebrated my precious son.

The gestures between cars would have brought a smile to most onlookers – and the "acceleration" button was used a few times . . . just to let the younger driver know "I got this!"

In need of caffeine – before entering the grounds, we stopped at one more Starbucks. This was a first – a mediocre Starbucks, that just couldn't get our order right. That challenge aside, we are so glad we stopped because – if it weren't for that stop we would not have landed… The. Best. Camping. Spot.

The grounds at *Summit Bechtel Reserve* (a 10,000-acre reserve) exceeded our expectations – truly a little piece of Heaven. Having arrived one day prior to the music festival beginning, and delayed with our coffee stop – we got the very last spot in the camping "lot" closest to the music grounds.

Our spot butted up against a hill, so we were able to position our vehicles and tents in a manner that provided this little haven within a haven.

Up went a one-person tent, the awning on the Land Cruiser, the ARB room off of the awning, the canopy, the hammock between the Land Cruiser and the pickup truck, and then the four-person tent. It almost felt like "glamping." Everyone was happy – the energy was perfect then – and for the whole adventure.

We brought all the food we would need for three days, and we ate well. Before we ate a late lunch that day, I presented the group with the "Full Send" shirts I had designed. The moment was perfect – they loved them. Ah, this mama's heart.

And, I just could not wait a moment longer – I set out the treasure hunt, and they searched and expressed delight just like Bryce would have. The clues lead them to bags filled with balsa airplanes, mini-flash lights, stickers, glow in the dark necklaces, paddle balls, and beach balls!

The paddle balls and beach balls fit right in with our games of cornhole and ring toss.

Included in the trip were two Origami bikes. These men, all avid mountain bikers, rode those bikes around the campsite area in such a fashion that now, I can't imagine a camping trip without them. They were both transportation and amusement as they performed tricks.

After searching for more ice – including a thirty-minute delay while a train made its way along the track and a short drive to try to locate the bike park – we had an incredible campfire meal of tacos. The conversation and humor lasted well into the night.

Morning brought with it a dense fog and temporary cool weather. I arose early – the showers were cold water dispensed with the pull on a chain – felt like I was back at a childhood campground. While my hair dried – I must have stood at the campsite for what seemed like an hour, watching the sun appear suddenly through the fog . . . tears flowing as I communicated with my precious Bryce. I thought I was alone at that early hour. I glanced over at a neighboring campsite and began a conversation with a woman there . . . in those brief moments we shared and shed more tears – the beginning of a beautiful friendship.

Then the campsite awoke – chatter could be heard coming from the tents scattered around. We settled into our own rhythm – a beautiful cadence of conversation and laughter. Our breakfast was incredible – the kind that can only be made over a camp stove. Little did I know, that we would need that energy. The decision was that we were going ziplining. I am very afraid of heights. That was the day I conquered a fear.

As we headed to the zipline site, I shared with the group that I had seen on the website that ziplining was an option and I had clicked right past it because, "there was no way I was going ziplining."

This young lady of perhaps 18 or 19 years of age, saw my fear, witnessed my tears, and committed to staying with me, triple-checking my gear, and encouraging me until "launch." The scariest moment was right at "launch" and then I felt Bryce right with me saying, "Full Send, mama – you got this." I was able to open my eyes and enjoy the ride.

I shared the accomplishment with Clare, and her response text in amazement was, "I sure hope someone got that on video!"

I kept telling myself and Bryce throughout the day, "I ziplined today."

That evening – the first concert night – sitting under the stars with a huge stage in front and people with incredible energy and kindness in the audience, one of the songs hit me deep in my heart and as I sat in my camp-chair, trying to make myself small as the tears flowed, not wanting to diminish the joy of others, Jake came from behind and enveloped me in a hug – a Bryce hug . . . no words, just understanding and love.

The music was incredible – deep, meaningful, the kind that reaches to the soul. There was worship in the music. Jake leaned over and stated, "I bet you did not think you would hear so many references to God and Jesus."

I may have been the first within our group that night to turn in as the others continued conversations around our mini-campfire, but I went to bed with a full heart.

The dawning of a new day began with rooster and chicken calls between the campsites – beginning a day with humor was new to me and so therapeutic. In fact, humor was part of the love language. Here were these precious young adults who each carried a part of Bryce with them; combined with their own uniqueness, I knew Bryce was present – the laughter, the conversation, the joking, the language, partaking in the things that Bryce liked, and the games . . . oh, the games – from pick-up-sticks, cornhole games, juggling, and ring toss, we added in sticker books and campfire cards – they were themselves, completely comfortable in my presence even though I am the age of their mothers – there was peace and happiness.

There was no judgment here – just people living . . . seemingly truly living – kindness was present.

Following a breakfast that surpassed any five-star restaurant, we ventured to the large pond located between our campsite and the performance area. Some rode bikes, and two of us hitched a ride in a side-by-side. The driver was in my age range and, along with his straw hat, wore a shirt with mushrooms, complemented with socks in the same design. As we raced along, the driver was trying to beat those on the bikes and yelling, "Watch yourselves, watch yourselves, sharks and fishes MF's . . ." The delivery was free-spirited and all in fun. The day was warm, and the water temperature was perfect. In the water, I was in my element – as the group jumped from the rocks and some swam to the other side of the pond, I was just happy to be in the water watching from afar. Once again, the humor continued . . . "What's your name?" "What?" "What is your name?" "Tony." Shouted from on top of the rocks. "F*** You, Tony! What's your name?" . . . "F*** You!" Was the communication shared. You had to be there.

The rest of the day was filled with the magic of more conversation, humor, games, and good food. That cornhole competition (the one with the new "man math" ha) – I am ready for the next round . . . you know who you are!

The last night of the concert was simply perfect. The outdoor venue was packed, yet there was breathing room, and the sounds of Arlo McKinley and Buffalo Wabs & the Price Hill Hustle filled the air. At one point, Casey Campbell with Buffalo Wabs said, "If you've lost someone, hold them up." As the tears flowed, I held up Bryce's obituary and gave the Full Send sign. The song that has been on repeat since we returned from the music festival is Buffalo Wabs' version of "The Very Best." The lyrics perfectly capture how I feel. "I might not be too good at most things I do; But I'm the very best at missing you." This is TRUTH - I may not be good at most things; I am the VERY BEST at missing Bryce. My heart remains shattered. Time now consists of trying to make it from one segment of time to the next.

The concert ended with an incredible performance by Tyler Childers on his Mule Pull Tour. The music, the message, the talent, the intensity . . . seemingly unsurpassable. The tears flowed freely during Tyler Childers' singing of "Follow You to Virgie." Bryce – I will see you soon.

Heading back to our campsite – knowing we had just witnessed amazing talent that touched us deeply, we longed to stop time . . . we did the best we could through the conversation shared around our mini-campfire.

"Is Katherine here?" It was 2:00 AM, and we were deep in conversation, and the precious new friend at the adjoining campsite stopped to share. Tyler Childers had encouraged the audience to reach out to at least one person in need. This lovely lady did just that . . . having been through some very challenging situations in her own life – experiencing grief on many levels, she got up the courage to reach out. I will forever be enriched by her kind gesture.

Early the next morning, I left the following message for the ladies in the nearby campsite. "Good Morning, Beautiful Women! Thank you for your kindness! You helped make this a special weekend. May your adventures together be full of wonder and celebration! We are strong women and can do AMAZING THINGS! Safe travels! With love, Katherine."

Breaking down the tents the final morning – even after the best omelets EVER, was just plain hard. The adventure had been perfect and now – the ARB camping room and awning, so loved by Bryce – were being packed away. I stepped into the camping room and as I shed a few tears, the question was posed by Jake, "Are you figuring out where to begin?" My reply, "Something like that." That was the safe reply – explaining how for weeks I had invested my thoughts into the planning for the trip, the hope it afforded, how it had held me together, and now facing the question of "What now?" Well, a quick reply was simpler – I still hesitated in showing that inside I was still completely losing it – that I wanted to scream LOUDLY, to rip my skin off, to plead and get my Bryce back – I would give anything . . . Such a response, though they would have enveloped me with love and care, is not considered polite company.

Five tired, happy people traveled home with vehicles packed to the brim, and a final Starbucks stop . . . at 3:33 PM – the hour of angel wings, we hugged good-bye and I got in my car to head back over the mountain with tears flowing – always feeling like I am leaving a part of Bryce on that side of the mountain.

A blanket of depression enveloped me during the two days following the festival. Now what?! Bryce is still not here. Why and how do I keep going?

God sent a sign – Bryce was being remembered even in a wedding in Hawaii. The feeding of a cardinal to begin the day. And, a priceless plaque with Bryce's pictures stood in witness to his love for the couple, Cody and Maddie, and their love for him. I treasured this love deep within my being.

A week after the festival, I joined the Whizzbangers Ball FB feed, and at the very moment that I needed, there was a picture of the message that I had left that last morning for the ladies. The comment was, "A huge thank you & sending love to Miss Katherine who camped next to us & left us this beautiful note. She lost her son & attended the festival with his friends. I would like to think Whizzbangers provided much needed respite &

healing for her. It was a privilege & honor to meet so many wonderful people." One of the responses was, "That's just the fellowship Tyler was hoping for. Love it."

Photographs of a butterfly landing on Jake's cycle and hand, ignoring all others in the group . . . twice in three days. A sign that Bryce was there.

Then there were the pictures sent of Luke sporting the Full Send hockey jersey while on his cycle and again on the top of Bryce's favorite mountain. "What would Bryce do?" Ah, this mama's heart.

For weeks, I had been watching for the line-up of Healing Appalachia. This week, on the date that marked the seventh month of Bryce's accident, I was at Bryce's gravesite and thought I will check again while here. The line-up had just dropped! – Absolutely, a sign that Bryce was with me. My heart was so full! I sent the message to the group! Yes, we will be going on another music/camping adventure . . . for Bryce!

A Visit by a Friend

Another ushering from one day to the next. Do you have time next week? Absolutely! Do you want to come here and stay for a day or more? A day reserved for just the two of us! Bryce's friend, Jenna, arrived with "Bryce Riverstone" (River) in tow – a beautiful six-month-old puppy named after Bryce. We grabbed Starbucks and ate breakfast with Bryce at his gravesite. The minutes turned into hours as we shared stories and "River" seemed to sense this was a very special spot –lying right next to the grave marker.

We followed with a hike along a stream, browsing in a country store, and lunch outside. The day continued from there – simply hours of conversation on the patio. The conversations were about Bryce as well as plans for our monthly adventures.

Age has no boundaries when it comes to grief and the extension of family members. This precious twenty-year old gave up a whole day to spend time with Bryce's mama. Also given was the stability of knowing others love Bryce, the hope generated knowing we have Bryce-related adventures on the horizon, and the comfort that my family now includes Bryce's friends.

Peach Picking

When Bryce was still in my womb, I turned for guidance to the book, *What to Expect When You're Expecting.* Chapter by chapter I could chart Bryce's expected growth and know what to anticipate with my changing body. Unlike a pregnancy book, there are no "guidebooks" that provide a roadmap of how to handle the passing of a loved one. Oh, there are many books on grief, but the variables present when losing a child are so vast that one book simply cannot capture the entire scope, as the age of the child, the circumstances around their passing, and the intricate nature of that child's relationship to the surviving parent and sibling are all elements of consideration.

Bryce, Bryce's sister, Clare, and I had a very special bond. Our little family had been through so much, and we were a tight-knit unit that moved in unison – sharing, protecting, and providing for each other. Without Bryce on this earth, there was no roadmap for moving forward. Clare and I are finding our way – it is painful. We are at different stages of grief and healing. There are times when my expressions – raw as they may be, and my sharing of Bryce are simply too overwhelming for Clare . . . tempering grief is not healthy, but sometimes necessary.

The question became, "How do we meet in a space that is healthy for both of us?" Our answer is to travel, explore, and create activities that are Bryce-related. This approach allows the creation of new memories, strengthening the bond between Clare and me, and the mutual sharing of aspects of the adventures that Bryce would love.

Yesterday, our exploration took us to Rappahannock County, Virginia, and the opening day of a farm offering "pick your own peaches." The day was a very hot 93 degrees. The farm was one of the most beautiful orchards we have seen – sprawling rows of peaches, nectarines, and apple trees set within the backdrop of the mountains. We were in a place Bryce would have loved seeing, mountains with which Bryce was very familiar. The skies were a royal blue with white clouds adding to the majesty.

With a box in one hand and our phones in the other, we picked peaches while capturing our laughter as we warded off the gnats and wondered at our sanity of picking fruit in the heat that made us feel like we were going to melt.

The few others in the orchards certainly did not know that mother and daughter – friends by heart – were working hard to create moments of beauty during life's most grueling turmoil.

No one bore witness to the shattered hearts – on the outside was laughter. We were trying.

Having filled our peach box, we added more magic to our day by going into town for lunch – the air-conditioned space a welcome respite.

Then, our exploration continued along a stream's path. While near the water, in a very private setting with the sun shining through the thick foliage, two butterflies danced together, encircling us again and again. We recognized what was occurring, and for those few moments time stood still as these black and blue Monarchs were delivering a message to us that Bryce is present. We cried and hugged each other tightly – priceless on so many levels.

We headed back on the path in search of an advertised apothecary. What we came upon in this wonderful town was an apothecary, a bakery, and a compilation of little shops. It was like discovering a little oasis of retail therapy where each shop was unique and a delight to experience. And, in the apothecary filled with all kinds of healing components, I came across a lotion – upon smelling it, my whole being wept; it smelled like Bryce. Bryce had used such a lotion. Another affirmation that Bryce was with us. I was meant to have that lotion.

The day was mother/daughter – friends . . . clinging to each other, searching for beauty in a very raw world. We were us. It was beautiful, memorable – somehow the day made us just a little stronger. Our hearts, and the many moments captured in photographs, bear witness to our courage and love.

Canandaigua Lake

Canandaigua Lake (the Lake) is Bryce's favorite place in the world. Like the mountains, it was his natural habitat. No formal training, yet Bryce could fly on water.

The Lake is where Bryce spent time almost every summer of his twenty-six years – though, due to COVID we missed the most recent years. It had been five years since I had traveled to the Lake (it, too, is where I had spent time almost every summer). I wrestled with whether the trip was prudent – considering both financial and workload factors – and decided I could not afford to not make the eight-hour journey. I traveled solo and met my daughter there. A little cottage right on the Lake. Every other time I had visited the Lake, I felt an anticipation of joy, like there was magic and celebration that awaited. This time, it was almost like feeling numb – my Bryce should have been there. I realized that seeing

the Lake through his eyes – the anticipation of his adventures was what made the Lake beautiful to me.

There were signs that Bryce was present. The first occurrence happened when I sat at the Lake, at the top of the stairs leading to the lakefront, watching the storm roll in, listening to the waves hit the shore, and feeling the wind.

I asked God to remove from me the spirit of performance. I then asked for a sign that Bryce is here and stated, "I know Bryce is here." At that moment an eagle flew right in front of me in the cove. I had never seen an eagle at the Lake. I was so moved I ran inside to tell Clare.

The second occurrence happened while I was rolling up an inflatable paddleboard that Bryce had used at his favorite Virginia lake. I was so thankful I was alone and could react unbridled. Bryce's handprints are on the underside of the paddle board – almost cemented there due to the red clay of Virginia. I could not breathe.

The third occurrence happened while I was searching the shoreline for sea glass. I decided to turn my search from sea glass to Indian heads (small rock formations that look like the top of a teepee and have indentations on them). I did not have any luck and was about to give up when I said, "Bryce would you just send a sign to me that you are

here by helping me find an Indian head?" Immediately, I found the most perfect Indian head, in size and color.

Dedication of Bryce's Plaque

Bryce had worked at Massanutten Resort for about six and one-half years. His resume stated the following:

> Lead Supervisor, manager on duty, lead bike mechanic, lead ski and snowboard technician, head of the trail crew to build, cut, grade, and maintain trails as well as erosion control, operator of excavators/machinery (certified rough terrain forklift operator), and emergency evac for the lift line. Supervised and managed up to twenty employees during the summer season, and up to one hundred employees over the course of the winter season, who were located in two buildings. Provided excellent customer service for all guests, as well as customers renting bikes, skis, and snowboards; during the winter season this service fluctuated between 1,200 – 3,000 people per day. Certified bike instructor, responsible for scheduling and running individual and group training sessions. Maintained mountain bikes, skis, and snowboards, including but not limited to rebuilding and swapping parts between machines. Ordered parts and supplies. Reconciled nightly cash register. Involved with multiple departments, including the opening and shutting down of mountain operations, and performing safety code and fire inspections throughout the resort. Cultivated and maintained relationships with industry leading companies, resorts, and community members.

The bike trails were his handiwork. Bryce loved that mountain. In August, eight months after Bryce's accident, Massanutten dedicated a plaque in Bryce's honor. The plaque is placed near the Summit, at the start of two bike trails, World Cup and All or Nutten. The plaque states, "We'll Meet Again on the Mountain. BRYCE RAY BRECKENRIDGE & HIS FULL SEND SPIRIT. 12/-3/1996 – 12/02/2023."

The weekend of the dedication was salve on this mama's heart. I spent time with Baylor riding around on the Gator, saw aspects of the trails that Bryce had designed and built, sat inside the old patrol cabin, and spent time at the Summit talking with Baylor about Bryce.

The group began arriving that night, and following another amazing dinner at Rocktown Kitchen, we stayed in a wonderful Airbnb. The next day began with our traditional Starbucks run (with a few

protesters heading to Chick-fil-A first) and unfolded from there on the grounds of Massanutten.

From the readying of bikes, the scenic lift tours, pictures at the Summit, food at Thirsty's, we moved as a group – loving Bryce, talking about Bryce, bringing his spirit with us. Then came the dedication of the plaque. People came from a wide range of places, including a very special mother and son who traveled quite a distance to honor Bryce. Bryce had taught the son for eight years how to mountain bike; Knox – you are very loved!

Walking Creamy – Bryce's favorite technical trail back to the Lodge with many who had ridden with Bryce, listening to stories of how Bryce encouraged others, taught technical approaches, and helped make building the trails and working in the tech shop (including the chocolate milk purchases) memorable – well those stories are treasured deep in this mama's heart. Closing the evening out at the Lodge and on the deck with pizza – Bryce's style, incredible company, and good music . . . Bryce is very loved.

The next day, cheering on many in Bryce's group who rode in Massanutten's "locals' race" was such a great privilege. Sporting Bryce's Full Send shirts and carrying his spirit – I know Bryce was the wind beneath their wheels.

Music for this Mama's Soul

Immediately following Bryce's accident, my existence went silent/dark for me. Time itself was painful. There simply was no oxygen. Somewhere in the periphery, I was aware of a flurry of people reaching out. There was no space in my world in which to receive any kindness. I just wanted Bryce back – nothing else mattered.

As time has passed, a numbness and despair have descended like a weighted, permanent cloak. The well-meaning outreaches have dwindled, and when they do occur, receiving is just too painful. Somehow in the rawness of loss, it is almost like kindness is a foreign feeling.

There are glimmers of hope – and to those I am holding on tight. One of Bryce's love languages, like mine, was the giving of gifts. That one perfect Christmas – when it was just Bryce and me – he shared a music genre that is now a lifeline for me. In Bryce's sharing, I am learning to find new places where my heart feels safe, where I know Bryce shows up – where his presence celebrates a new freedom alongside me.

Seeking those moments - Buffalo Wabs & The Price Hill Hustle was playing at Bright Box in Winchester. I did not feel well, but there was no way I was going to miss hearing this incredible band live. Baylor, Jenna, and I got perfect seats with an unobstructed view of the stage in a theater that has somewhat of a warehouse feeling. The setting is sparse and is ideal as the focus is on the talent.

As we waited for the first band, I could see that Casey Campbell and Buffalo Wabs were in the foyer. I handed my backpack to Baylor, gathered my courage, and asked if I could introduce myself. I explained how their song, "The Very Best," is my favorite song and how it perfectly captures how I feel about my son, Bryce, who passed away in a horrific motocross accident just eight months ago. I shared that the lyric, "I might not be too good at most things I do; but I'm the very best at missing you," is how I feel about myself and Bryce. To this aching mama's heart, it felt like Casey Campbell heard me, saw me – that he recognized loss and deep sorrow.

Following a great opening band, Buffalo Wabs & the Price Hill Hustle took the stage, and what I heard was like a feast for my ears and senses. The talent, message, and heart in their performance feel almost unsurpassable. As they neared the end of the show, Casey Campbell introduced their next song, "The Very Best." Though he did not use a name, I believe his message was for Bryce and me, and as he shared, he placed his hand on his heart. I wept and offered the Full Send sign for Bryce – it was one perfect moment in a time when life is very raw and horrible, during which someone heard my heart – touched my pain in a way that few are able, and for that I am so very and forever grateful. I would have traveled across the nation for just that moment.

When the band finished, I saw Casey Campbell remove his earpiece and walk towards the foyer. I looked at Baylor and Jenna and said, "I am going in that direction if you want to join me." As I walked towards the foyer, Casey Campbell walked towards me and gave me the most genuine hug. It was a hug that said, "I know. I see." There are no more words needed.

Healing Appalachia

A Road to Recovery . . . From a Shattered Heart

The music sweeps over one in waves – healing waves, in which the lyrics speak truth/tell stories/reach deep into one's heart. The demands/commotion/variables of the world are left on the other side of the entrance. Judgment and controversy are not welcome. The focus of the healing is on those who have struggled with addiction – for this mama, the music, the atmosphere, the camaraderie, the safe place to "just be," served as one step in this horrible journey of grief.

Planning for the music festival helped me move from one day to the next. Checking my list of "camping gear," readying the "travel/treat bags," and planning the treasure hunt – somehow, I made it to the day of the "road trip."

The five of us – this time it was Baylor, Jenna, Cody, Maddie, and me. After a food run to Chick-fil-A, the "travel/treat bags" were a hit – filled with items loved by Bryce – Oreos, Animal Crackers, Turkish Taffy, and PEZ candy. The bingo cards were handed out, and our three-car caravan

headed towards West Virginia in the rain. Tyler Childers was our music of choice – Bryce's genre!

Stopping at the rest area before the state fairgrounds, Cody won the prize for bingo: 686 Grateful Dead coasters. We then made our way through beautiful downtown Lewisburg and to the entrance of the fairgrounds. Arriving early enough to be choosy about our campsite, we picked well and set up our home away from home. The guys took care to set up the awning and "camping room" first and then my tent. Once all tents, awnings, decorative lights, tables, games, and fire pit were in place, I gave the gang the "Full Send" shirts I had made in honor of Bryce. We then made our first Walmart run – of course. That Walmart run was one for the memory books. We purchased little, green foam men that cautioned, "Slow down, Kids at Play." We placed those and "Slow Down, We ♥ Our Children" signs along the perimeter of our campsite.

The next morning, I set up the treasure hunt clues – something I always did for Clare and Bryce at each holiday/event. The items to be found this time were all items loved by Bryce: marshmallow skewers, bubblegum-flavored Jelly Belly packets, balsa airplanes, metal slinkies, bounce pinky balls, stickers, pins, Bazooka Bubble Gum, and Hot Wheels Toyota Land Cruisers (if you know, you know). The treasure hunt was a hit!

We then needed to escape the heat, so a Starbucks run was next. While there, we walked around Downtown Lewisburg. Our first stop was a "Surf Shop." The owner is wonderful and a supporter of Healing Appalachia – he had even designed wool jackets for Tyler Childers and Senora May. We then ventured through gift and vintage shops. Jenna found wonderful white, vinyl dress boots and "rocked" them along with her new, short-sleeve cow shirt on the first concert night.

We were joined that afternoon by friends of Maddie – Julie, and her daughter, Emily. You know when you meet someone and instantly you recognize they will be friends for life – that's Julie and Emily. They fit into our little group perfectly.

Each musical festival provides an opportunity for an introduction to amazing talent new to me. The latest gems discovered this time were Sierra Ferrell and My Morning Jacket.

My very favorite picture is Cody on my right and Baylor on my left – our backs to the camera . . . during My Morning Jacket's performance – it was like being surrounded by Bryce.

As a means of thanking Casey Campbell for his kindness in Winchester and in honor of Bryce, I had brought a "Full Send" shirt to give to Casey Campbell along with a card and note about how much the music of Buffalo Wabs & The Price Hill Hustle means to me. The first full day at Healing Appalachia, I sent a FB Message to Casey Campbell asking if there was a means I could present the gift to him during the music festival. He responded with their travel plans and said he looked forward to meeting during the festival. For this mama's heart that is so full of hurt, the kindness – the being seen – is so very precious.

The music, the memories made with Bryce's group, and being able to present a gift and message in honor of Bryce – the moments helped hold me together.

Bryce's Signature

Never did I understand until now, the meaning a tattoo can have. In fact, there was a time in my life when I was adamant, "not me." I had thought about this for months, and it was on my "list" of things I wanted to do for Bryce in 2024. One Saturday, Clare and I just decided that today is the day. We had Bryce's signature, and the words "FULL SEND" tattooed on our left forearms.

Sitting in Silence

Tomorrow marks nine months since you walked this earth. It is not lost on me the significance that I carried you inside of me for nine months and that utter joy, contrasted with nine months of the most excruciating pain, despair, and sorrow one could know. The space in between – the moments during each day that were filled with our conversations as well as the shared silence – just glad to be in each other's presence/knowing how to be in each other's presence . . . all of it is just silence now. I am told to find a hobby, join a book club, invite someone for coffee – this list goes on – none of it seems like a welcome venture. I would rather sit in my silence – in this deep pit of pain and think about you than have even the most well-meaning conversation fill the space.

I have voiced, "I can work, but I don't like life." I said what I said. When dawn arrives each day, I state three things: "F#*!, I'm still here?" "How am I going to make it through today?" And, "Lincoln, mommy loves you and Bryce loves you."

Bryce's Heart

I knew Bryce's heart, his precious - pure heart.

When I share with others that I just want Bryce back, that I beg God to bring him back, the response I often receive is, "It doesn't work that way; that's not God's plan." Or, "I can't ask God to do that for you."

How do they know? Perhaps this sentiment comes from a mama's heart that is so full of pain that it takes this level of discouragement and despair to ask the hard question(s). WHY NOT!?!!!! Why can't IT work that way? My God, who has all authority, is my son's Creator, who let Bryce be born, who chose the date and time that Bryce was taken from this earth . . . He most certainly can choose to bring him back. Why do the others limit my God and draw the line, saying, "That's not how it works?" Miracles – if they exist, and I believe they do . . . why not bring Bryce back? I want my son back. I want my son back NOW! Do they say such statements because they have a limited belief in the authority of my God? Is it because such a response places my God in a neat little box? Is it because they have not seen such a miracle with their own eyes, and they are afraid that if they pray for Bryce's return to me and it doesn't happen it will confirm their own shaky foundation of faith?

My world stopped when Bryce's accident occurred. Moving through each day feels like I am moving through the murkiest, thickest sludge. The world expects too much from me. I am not sure how or why the world keeps on going. Do they not know that my precious Bryce is now in a different realm? How does everyone not know that this perfect man is no longer here?

A week ago, five and a half months after Bryce's accident, my cousin called and beautifully shared his condolences and love, and he also stated he had just found out that Bryce had passed.

Deep feelings of sadness, as well as anger surfaced . . . HOW in any creation is that possible?

Did my son not mean enough, was he not important enough that someone would have told my cousin this life-changing news?

How can a mama be expected to "adjust" to her child not being here on this earth? I love being Bryce's mama. I am now no longer sure what that is supposed to look like. It's the big things and the little things that shake my world – that are the stark reminders that life is not as it should be. Even going into a grocery store is painful. My cart is no longer filled with Bryce's favorites – Ragu pizza sauce, frozen cheese pizza, pasta, Horizon 2% milk, baguettes, and Jiff peanut butter. The evening silence is present where our conversations and Facetimes once were. The checkerboard and pickup sticks sit in the game basket unattended. Even my piano remains silent – joy is not showing its face. The calls stating, "I am one mile away, can you open the gate?" – no longer occur. The statement, "I'll be back." – no longer true.

A favorite book of Bryce's when he was little was, *The Kissing Hand*. We followed suit, and when he was younger, we would place a kiss in the palm of each other's hand. We did that a few times recently – it was always a promise that he would return. Recently, I re-read the book. When I got to the very last page, I lay on the ground and wept – there on that last page was the symbol representing FULL SEND and love. It is not by chance that this was Bryce's favorite book – I believe he knew that somewhere in time I would need a message from him, and there it was.

A mom is supposed to protect her child – anticipate any harm that may come their way. The feeling like I have failed . . . it is overwhelming. I did not even get to say, "goodbye."

I lose track of days/time. Grief takes up a lot of my bandwidth. There is no sleep . . . and, when morning arrives – sometimes I find myself choking or weeping and my first thought is, "I'm still here?" And, then the reprocessing of this nightmare I am living. The question persists – How do I make it through the day?

BRYCE'S HEART

I knew Bryce's heart, his precious - pure heart.

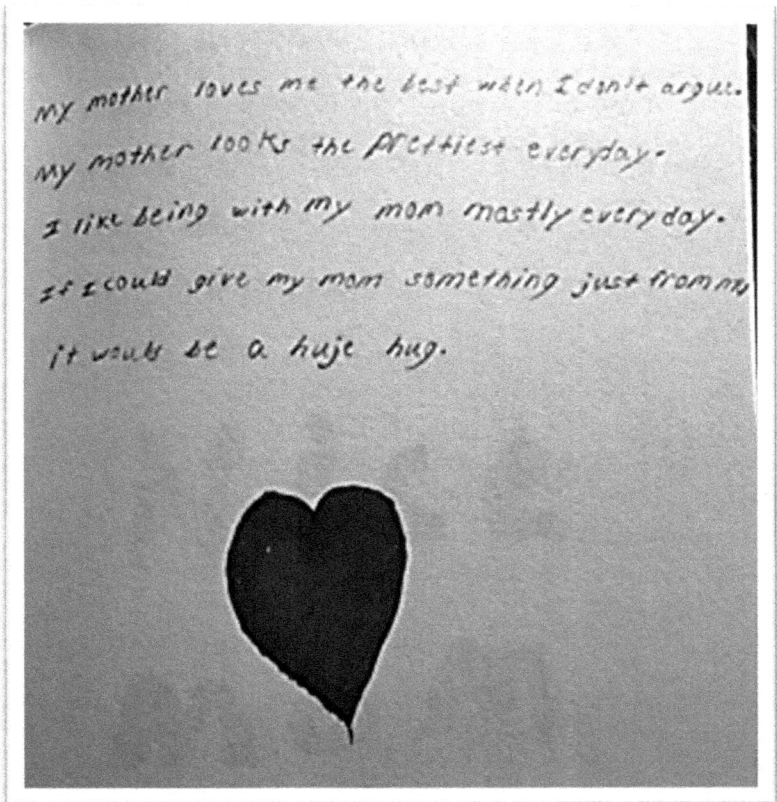

By Bryce – In Elementary School

Anxiety and Isolation

I have found that grief is not an emotion that stands alone. Grief has some nasty tentacles. One of those is anxiety.

The knowledge that bad things, horrific things do happen and can happen to me, makes the ring of the phone, loud yelling, stress, road rage, and reports of bad news all triggers. I don't want the phone to ring – I don't want a knock on my door.

I know I need to be around humans – that would be healthy, but few will ever understand the pain I am living . . . so, isolation is my fortress. There is no "welcome" place. I look for Bryce everywhere.

The strength and grace of my daughter, Clare – sister to Bryce, has been amazing. We grieve differently. She has been strong when I could not be. From the moment I learned of Bryce's accident, Clare stepped in and surrounded me with a veil of protection. It was Clare who made the phone calls, sent text messages, made sure there was food in the house, interacted with visitors, put in place elements of protection, and created pathways so that I could grapple with the suffocating pain.

It was Clare on whom I leaned. She became my touchstone – letting me know there was a constant human. As the service and celebration became days in the past, Clare let me know daily when I would see her, and she reserved her break at work so that we could sit together for that half hour in the parking lot, just so I would know some stability.

Slowly, Clare began adding elements of beauty back into my world. Her own birthday arrived so closely to Bryce's passing that we were both numb that day and stayed within the safety of our four walls. My birthday was not far enough away either; however, Clare coordinated a gathering with Bryce's core group, and I could feel Bryce's presence. The gift was priceless. Being in Bryce's places with Bryce's core group – this is when my smile is genuine.

Recently, Clare's place of work publicized an article about Clare. Initially, when Clare sent a copy to me, I thought the focus was strictly promotional for the gym. When I read it, the gift of love embedded in the article wrapped its arms around me and took my breath away. In the middle of the article, my daughter wrote, "My mom is my biggest inspiration in life. She has faced levels of adversity that most can't begin to imagine, but she has still found the strength to continue to show up every day and has been the best mom my brother and I could have asked for. I try to model how I show up for myself and my clients by the way she has always shown up. She is the strongest woman I know and is an inspiration to me every day."

Yesterday, Clare shared with me that for an upcoming trip, she and her boyfriend will be putting together a treasure box for his daughter. "We are going to do a prize/treat box for the road trip to the beach for his daughter, like you did for us growing up! Thank you for doing that for us 💜 I'm able to share it now, which is cool." Ah, this mama's heart.

95

Counseling Sought

For five years, I have received weekly counseling from an extraordinary counselor. I have poured out my heart, my trials, and my accomplishments. She is beautifully gifted at gently coaching me in the healing process following stepping into a world that fostered the already tight bond shared between my children and me. She has become my friend and confidant – providing a safe place of expression. Even though I place my deepest heart matters before this trusted person, three months after Bryce's accident, we both recognized that seeking counsel from one who is skilled at grief trauma counseling would be imperative for me to not remain completely consumed with grief and despair. The signs were apparent to me that I desperately needed help.

There are many grief counselors; however, finding a counselor who provides grief trauma counseling is challenging. I made inquiries across the country (all the way to Arizona) and was unable to establish a solid connection. Some had full client schedules, and others were not set up to conduct telehealth sessions. I had almost resolved that I would have to "save" myself – that somehow, I was once again going to have to work my way out of a very dark hole.

I do not believe the following was coincidental (nor do I believe in coincidences). On this particular day, I ventured into Walgreens, a store I may frequent once a year. Going out into the public takes a lot of courage and energy when one is consumed by grief. I wish I had a shield that would make me invisible. People can be very kind, but the grief hurts so badly that interacting with others in the early stages is just plain hard. This errand began the same as all others – I hung my head and "stayed on task," hoping to have enough courage and stamina to get the item I needed and get safely back into my car. I was in the check-out line and a dear friend, who I have not seen in years, but our children were on swim team together, graced me with a huge hug, a warm heart, conversation about Bryce, and she dove right in and committed to finding a grief trauma counselor for me. She did just that. She searched and searched. She found not just one, but three, and all fairly local to me.

I reached out to one, located about half an hour from me, but lost my courage and cancelled before we even met. In her kind email reply, she shared that she, too, had lost a son. I felt my world spin as the revelation that she, too, would know such pain hit so close to home.

During this timeframe, I reached out to another counselor recommended by my friend, already knowing that he had experienced the loss of a child. In fact, my precious Bryce had been friends with his child, making the connection feel safe. In response to my text message inquiry, his immediate phone call prompted me to commit to the first counseling session.

Session One

During the first session, I shared a lot – setting the stage for this counselor to provide guidance as I placed the complexities of my grief in his hands. I shared the three prongs of my trauma – with the most horrific of all being the passing of precious Bryce. I tried to describe my shattered heart, to verbalize my despair, to capture the utter silence while simultaneously remaining in a deafening tailspin. I spoke of the extreme fatigue and body aches, of somehow putting on my black suit and pearls and being able to take care of client matters, and of the weeping and screams that commence in the silent moments. The counselor listened way beyond the allotted time. As the session ended, he gave me three tasks: (1) pray to God to give me understanding, (2) ask Bryce to petition God for the same, and (3) "schedule" time for the "extreme expressions" of grief (I learned this (discipline of the mind) also in law school – scheduling time to worry about Clare and Bryce; it was essential in order to pass my classes and the Bar) – that is a work-in-progress I think forever.

I understand why the counselor recommended these three steps. Since Bryce's accident, my relationship with God seemed to come to an abrupt standstill. It is like for all of my life God has been with whom I have spoken, my foundation, the very reason for my being, and the rock on whom I placed ALL. Before December 2nd – that most HORRIBLE DAY – I spoke with God constantly throughout my days. Now, I don't even know what to say – and I am wrestling with whether He is even listening. So, I started with step one. As I sit beside Bryce's gravesite every day, I offer this one simple prayer asking God to provide me with an understanding of why this happened, why He allowed Bryce to be taken from this earth? I know this prayer, though it seems a simple task and prayer without much fanfare, it is a complex stepping-stone to opening up the communications between God and me of seemingly bygone days. Interlaced in my conversations with Bryce while at his gravesite (all the while sitting there aching – wanting to dig up his grave just so I can touch his hands once again) is my request of Bryce that he petition Jesus to give me understanding of why this happened. The third task is the hardest. I have spent five and a half months crying and screaming – in complete anguish when others are not nearby. Instead of a scheduled "time" of day during which to express my grief, I have chosen Bryce's gravesite to be my "place" of expression, a visit to which happens each day at varying times.

This third step will forever be a work-in-progress. The grief bursts arise seemingly out of nowhere – triggered by a picture, a memory, a sound, a smell, a thought of what should be . . . Twenty-four hours a day, I miss Bryce to my core, and the shroud of grief from within and without is ever present. I am trying and will continue to try to turn the other twenty-three hours into ones during which conversations with Bryce occur, ones during which I don't tunnel down into the depths of despair, but instead are ones from which I lean in and listen to what Bryce is teaching me, what he wants to show me, the adventures on which he wants me to embark.

Before I left the first session, the counselor made a statement that I interpreted as follows. Because of Jesus's pain, God has felt my suffering – but for it, my suffering for Bryce would be for naught – that God would not be a God of understanding/compassion.

Grappling with grief is painful work.

Between the first and second weeks of meeting with the counselor, the first suggested counselor – who I had not met, sent an email recommending the book, *Lament for a Son*, by Nicholas Wolterstorff. The few nights I spent reading this book from cover to cover found me exclaiming, "He gets it." "This sounds like my story." While weeping and screaming because it is so on point. Read. This. Book.

Session Two

In the second counseling session, I spent the first forty-five minutes in tears reading through the highlights in *Lament for a Son*. What hit me initially was how similar our sons' accidents were and how we heard of their passing. Then concepts ran in parallel: taking for granted one's child would always be present, the gift of a child who has been snatched away, now there is a void, wanting to turn back the hands of time, the beauty of this world is no more, protection of a child, and the wrestling of a bereaved parent regarding God, death, and WHY.

I wept as I spoke of the parallels. My emphasis kept returning to the WHY and my relationship with God. The faith I had always known, that had been the sustaining grace and foundation, where was it now? It felt so distant. God felt so distant. Everything felt so distant, but the grief. The grief – it is there at dawn, punches you in the gut throughout the day, and settles like a weighted blanket on you in the evening hours. I explained how I was trying to work my way back to the Truth; that I recognized that I needed the Truth; that I felt like I was operating in a vacuum. I have just me.

During the session, the counselor said that God may be teaching me how to listen better to Him. My response was that I have always communicated with God – that it was a two-way conversation. He asked what I have always equated God to. My response was Joy. He added that God is so much more – one of those aspects is sorrow – that God experienced sorrow when Christ died. Again, he stated that God will use Bryce's passing for good. In this "stage of trying/learning" my response was, Jesus was King – in my mind, that was enough – that was the accomplishment; Bryce was not a king, and his passing was too high a price. You can sense the pain and anguish in this mama's heart. The "why" my child?!?

Towards the end of the session, the counselor tasked me with forgiving God . . . SO MANY layers of complexity with all of this. The counselor explained that I had put God in a box, the same way I had put other people who had wronged me into boxes. I explained that it was part of my survival mode. I could still be civil – behave as required – but was forewarned and forearmed, with boundaries in place.

The counselor – who has let me know he is a Catholic, and to that I shared that I was raised Baptist/Presbyterian/and non-denominational, interlaces his sharing with Biblical foundations to which I am clinging so that I can find my footing – so that I can work my way back to the Truth – so that I gain some understanding. He tried to allay my fears of Bryce not being okay. He said that Bryce no longer needed human help because he is in Heaven and there is no pain in Heaven, or it wouldn't be Heaven. When I asked about Bryce hearing me, he referenced Revelation and John watching the smoke rise from the incense – prayers from the people on earth. The counselor spoke of Moses and Elijah on the mountain, conversing with Jesus after they had died.

The beautiful gem of wisdom, which the counselor shared and I am holding onto the most, is that Bryce is now in a more powerful, complete form than we can conceptualize, and that he can't fade – that he will never fade.

Session Three

What do you think of when you think of Heaven?

> Love. Pure love.

Where do you think Bryce is now?

> In Heaven.

Bryce is now eternally connected to God.

> But, as his mama, it was always my job to protect Bryce – to make sure he had what he needed – to keep him safe.

Bryce can now take care of Bryce.

Bryce is now more powerful than he ever was.

Bryce is no longer constrained by time or space.

Session Four

I have expanded my prayer from "please give me understanding" to "please give me understanding, peace, and trust." They are so intertwined for me.

Bryce only shows up at the gravesite when you are there.

Now, Bryce and I go to the gravesite together – we sit together at the place where his physical body is at rest. And, we leave together.

Session Five

Miracles, signs, and wonders. Those moments that have been considered "but, God" moments – they are miracles. They are designed and set forth by God to let me know He is still there, that He still sees me.

Your faith is growing/going deeper.

I no longer listen to "traditional worship" songs. I find Bryce and worship in songs that I would deem "alternative," bluegrass, folk, and "Appalachian." Right now, the words of deep faith and life's challenges touch deep in my soul.

The Grace and Love of My Sister

My sister, Sallie, has been a rock for me in my world that is upside/down. She has walked alongside me during the roughest of times – she has been steadfast and shown up daily with grace and love. In addition to my daughter, she is the smartest, kindest, most insightful/giving/beautiful woman I know. We spoke of the counseling sessions, and she added a God-level to this process that I had not seen.

"THESE ARE ALL GOD THINGS" – as my sister pointed out.

The office complex in which the counseling sessions are held is one which my energy has resisted going to for years, yet I went.

The counselor's office is small with outdated furniture – in fact, there was popcorn on the floor, yet I welcome this over a sterile, cold atmosphere in which I might be just a number.

The counselor is Catholic – I am not . . . we both love the Lord. He hears me, sees me, remembers the points I have made, and has a brilliant mind. He presents strong, foundational, Biblical support for the guidance he is sharing with me.

. . . The popcorn – my family loves popcorn . . . it is now on the floor.

Welcome Home Bike

Bryce is known to have been the best bike mechanic at Massanutten. This mama treasures every item that Bryce's hands touched.

On November 16th, I welcomed home a TREK full suspension bike that Bryce had worked on and Massanutten had decommissioned. That bike is positioned near Bryce's favorite bike, and daily I hug both.

A Year Makes its Turn . . .

Every moment of that week – one year ago, I remember it as if it were yesterday. It was the week after Thanksgiving. Bryce and I worked on his resume that Sunday – the experience and skill he had to offer read like a poem. We sat for hours in this very living room as we conversed about his expertise.

Of course, neither of us knew that within a few days, Bryce would be joining the "Angel Band." Now, I sit in the same space – numb and in deep pain at the same time. I have done everything I know to do, and yet still, Bryce is not walking through the door. How in the world will I make it through another day, another 365 days?

November 30

Clare and I had made plans to spend two nights in West Virginia prior to celebrating Bryce's birthday. We reserved an Airbnb, which is located in the basement of a bike shop – the perfect Airbnb in Bryce's memory. West Virginia had a winter storm come through, and Clare and I changed our plans – as much as we love West Virginia, we wanted to make sure we could make it to Harrisonburg on December 2nd for the gatherings with the core group.

We arrived in Harrisonburg two nights earlier than planned. The weather was in the teens, and staying near our "destination" was a good decision. It allowed us to settle in, to purchase the last-minute items for the up-coming gatherings, and to spend time just the two of us. We also had fun exploring the Green Valley Bookfair and waiting for the perfect hamburgers to be ready at Thirsty's – worth it!

December 1

In search of creating traditions of our own, Clare and I attended a Christmas festival at a farm way out in the country where local artisans were present, Christmas trees were being sold, and musicians entertained. The setting was magical, and Bryce sent snow flurries.

Both days were "book-ended" with Starbucks coffee and Insomnia Cookies!

December 2

I remember every single moment of this day a year ago – the worst day EVER!!! Time felt like 365 days had not passed. What I knew was that I needed to be at The Summit at Massanutten no later than 1:30.

Clare, Cody, Kolten, Baylor, Luke, Knox, Kim, and I braved the wind and cold that day. As we stood at The Summit, overlooking the valley below, at 1:44 I read a poem I had written about Bryce and presented each person with "pocket coins" on which Bryce's favorite Bible verses were imprinted. As I shared, the skies opened, rays of sunshine poured down, and the image of the cross appeared. Bryce was most definitely present.

I then gave a photo album to each person. The album contained pictures of Bryce that were familiar to the core group and pictures of the core group over the last twelve months as we tried to gain our footing.

That evening, Clare, Cody, Maddie, Ryker, Kolten, Baylor, Jenna, Luke, Knox, Kim, and I gathered at Reddish Knob. In the freezing cold, we celebrated Bryce as we watched the setting sun – with candles, toasts, sparklers, "BRB" in gold, the burial of private words in a cherry box, and the giving of gifts.

To: Cody and Maddie – a 686 Grateful Dead blanket – Bryce would have loved it!
To: Cody – a stained-glass FULL SEND sign – Bryce knew!
To: Bryce's Core Group – A Leather Journal

To: Treasured Friends –
Who Each Carry a Part of Bryce with Them

The following is the entry Bryce made in his journal on November 24, 2023, one week prior to the accident.

Bucket List – Overland/ride dual sports through the Andes Mountain Range.

Enclosed is a journal – perhaps in which you can write a Bucket List.

Daily, as I think, "What Would Bryce Do?" I have been challenging myself to keep going – well, I know Bryce would want me/us to do "more than keep going." One of my mentors once encouraged me to write down the biggest dream I had and then tear up that paper and let God do something even bigger. Right now, finding some semblance of stability seems to be the challenge, but I am certain that Bryce would want each of us to dream big, REALLY BIG!

Let's create a core group bucket list and live, LIVE BIG – for Bryce!

Core group Bucket List – For Bryce

Bryce Started It –	Overland/ride dual sports through the Andes Mountain Range
	Canandaigua Lake
	Colorado
	Utah – Salt Flats and Moab
	Splinters Boardshop in Warren, VT
	Ray's Indoor Bike Park
	Montana
	Swiss Alps
I'll Add to It –	Establishment of a Foundation in Honor of Bryce

With love,
Katherine – Bryce's Mama

December 3

Bryce's birthday – Born at 9:30 in the morning. How are you not here on what would be your twenty-eighth birthday?

To celebrate you – we gathered at Magpie's Diner. Present were Clare, Cody, Maddie, Ryker, Baylor, Jenna, Jake, McKenna, and I. – We showed up in our sweatshirts that honor Bryce. While waiting for our breakfast, we played a Bryce Trivia Game. I lined the top of the table with gift bags, each filled with contents that Bryce would have loved . . . marbles, bubblegum in a roll, knives (huge shout out to Pete and Samantha from The Bear and The Blade), Dr. Squatch soap . . .

The following were the trivia questions:

(1) What was Bryce's first word?
(2) Bryce's two favorite colors?
(3) What sport did Bryce play in high school?
(4) The name of the shop where Bryce had his first job?
(5) Name Bryce's three main foods. (pizza, pasta, French fries.)
(6) What was Bryce's favorite TV show growing up?
(7) What is the name of Bryce's pasta sauce?
(8) What did Bryce have to do prior to eating at a new restaurant?

When the food (an amazing meal) arrived, I shared part of a short story I had written about Bryce and presented the group with an ornament with the stenciled image of Bryce mountain biking and the words "FULL SEND" on it.

I also presented puzzles with images of snow-covered mountains and people skiing.

From there, Clare, Baylor, Jenna, River (Baylor and Jenna's dog named after Bryce – Bryce Riverstone), and I went to Switzer Lake. In Bryce's favorite location on the lake, in very cold weather with snowflakes gracing us, we decorated the spot with cloth banners, we roasted marshmallows over a campfire, had a treasure hunt (all items honoring Bryce), and ate cake. Before departing, Clare and I disbursed the ashes of Conrad – our very special dog loved by Bryce – in a spot we know Bryce loved.

Baylor, Jenna, and I ended the evening at Rocktown Kitchen – a tradition . . . a place to gather – good food, incredible people – in honor of Bryce.

CHRISTMAS ARRIVES AGAIN

Christmas Eve – our little family trying hard to be present for each other in the midst of the raw pain of missing Bryce's presence . . . the Saran Wrap ball game filled with camping items and gift cards – all items Bryce would have loved, brought forth beautiful laughter – from Clare as Starbucks gift cards were revealed, and then from my parents when bear bells fell from the plastic wrap. The evening came to a close with the traditional Christmas Eve gift presentation – this time it was a Christmas flannel shirt, one that would have been a favorite of Bryce's.

Christmas Morning – As we all sported our new flannel shirts during the exchange of gifts, I unabashedly played Tyler Childers' Feathered Indians, and stood and wept – that is Bryce's and my Christmas song . . . and, my heart was breaking.

Keeping with tradition – the sharing of gifts was followed by a treasure hunt, which included items loved by Bryce – fudge, chocolate coins, popcorn . . . bringing delight to my parents upon each find; I could sense Bryce's beautiful smile as no matter the age, a treasure hunt was always a welcome highlight.

Halfway through the day, I crawled back into bed – and slept . . . there was no joy.

Time in the Mountains

It is not lost on me that Bryce's soul changed realms while he was in West Virginia, and some of Bryce's favorite places were in its mountains.

I had received an alert that Buffalo Wabs & the Price Hill Hustle would be playing at The Purple Fiddle in Thomas, West Virginia, just before the new year. Anticipating the transition – that the days following Christmas would be challenging, Clare and I decided that making a trip into the mountains to be with Bryce's spirit would be well-timed.

The holiday moments have been wrought with waves of deep despair, and I have struggled to find my footing. Knowing that I would be able to hear Buffalo Wabs & the Price Hill Hustle was somewhat of a lifeline for me. In addition, the preparation of a gift for Casey Campbell and his family – items locally made in Virginia, as well as pocket coins of Bryce's two favorite Bible verses – provided glimpses of happiness.

As Clare and I traveled into the mountains on that Friday, Bryce's spirit was right alongside us as the beauty engulfed us.

We arrived during the late afternoon, and before checking into our Airbnb in Thomas, West Virginia, Clare and I found a wonderful restaurant in Davis, West Virginia. Hellbender Burritos was a MUST EAT AT place! The food was incredible, and the atmosphere was relaxed in an eclectic way. We ate there twice during the weekend. And, what a memory-making weekend it was. Hellbender Burritos has since closed its doors, so Clare and I will be in search of another perfect restaurant.

Oh, Purple Fiddle, you did not disappoint.

Oh, Purple Fiddle, you did not disappoint.
    After months of waiting –
        this mama ran down the sidewalk.
    Dark – Rain – a gift in hand, and finally a smile.
Inside – kindness, acceptance.
    There was another who had lost a child –
        that moment of recognition.
    Tender connection.
Then the one who sees the deep sorrow –
    for him I have a mere present.
The stage welcomed the greatest of talent –
    Buffalo Wabs & the Price Hill Hustle.
Music and message in which this mama's heart finds
    Community.
    Understanding.
    Safety.
    Hope.
It is one step to the next step.
    For in those moments, I was not alone.
    Steadying.
    Reassuring.
    Encompassing.
        Priceless gifts.
A full heart – even as the night is old.
    Rich, wonderful coffee in this magical, eclectic town.
    Free – little libraries.
    Art abounds.
    Placement of wisdom plaques extraordinaire.
    Welcomed anonymity.
Now, mountain bound.
Dolly Sods.
    Conquering Fears.
    Inflated tires.
        Mud.
        More mud.
        Snow.
        Rocks.

Steep inclines.
So worth the traverse.
Rock formations.
Mountain views.
Deep valleys.
Bryce's spirit – very present . . . and, the skies opened.
The exploration continued . . . White Grass.
Unassuming place with the most welcoming heart.
Cross-country skiing.
Happy adventurers.
Bryce's go-to spot for split-boarding.
Bryce is teaching me how to live . . .
Mama's spot for cross-country skiing and
snowshoeing.
Treasured snowshoes outfitted by Chip himself
– and they still have a little "White Grass
magic" on them.
Hellbender Burritos
So great we had to return!
Sleep
What's sleep when one has one more day to explore?
Coffee
When you find "That Spot" – one called "Tip Top,"
enter that door/buy the coffee!
Blackwater Falls
Majestic.
Awesome.
Painted by fallen needles.
Produces its own music.
Not created by chance.
Home
Familiar.
Quiet.
Alone.
Still waiting.

The transition from time spent over the mountain to time in Bryce's beloved spaces has proven challenging. A deep depression – like a weighted blanket – descends. I have given all, and still Bryce is not here. My way of gaining a foothold, aside from planning for the next trip over the mountain, is to give gifts.

Upon returning home from the weekend in the Thomas-Davis, West Virginia Area, I did what I know best. I gave gifts. I mailed leather journals – the same ones used by Bryce for his bucket list – to the members of Buffalo Wabs & the Price Hill Hustle. Included in the mailing were details of Bryce's bucket list and the draft chapter about the Thomas-Davis, West Virginia, weekend trip. The following is the personal message written to the band.

To: Matt Wabnitz, Casey Campbell, Scott Risner, Bill Bablock, and Brian Iles:

Thank you so very much for an AMAZING show at the Purple Fiddle! Thank you for sharing your talents and providing a space that is transformative for those in attendance. The moments were magical for this hurting mama's heart. I am very grateful.

Enclosed in this box is a small gift for each of you that comes with lots of love. I presented one to each person in Bryce's core group . . . perhaps they will provide some inspiration to you, too.

With love,
Katherine Breckenridge – Bryce's Mama

New Year's Eve

I spent the evening simply communicating with Bryce. The time was beautiful, painful, lonely, healing, raw . . . moments that were priceless – there was no other way I would have chosen to spend the time. Truly, what is the point of a new year? My reasons for being have shifted. Still, I tried – tried to keep moving forward, placed goals in front of me; that's what Bryce would want.

I wrote five bucket lists and a declaration page.

Bryce Bucket List 2025

Finish writing and publishing my book.
Breckenridge Nomadics/BRB Foundation
Muscle Building
Ride the trails.
Downhill ski with the skis from Bryce.
Snowboard.
Snowshoe with shoes from White Grass.
Cross-country ski more.
Passport
Overland Expo.
Kayak more.
Buy land.
Whizzbangers Ball.
Healing Appalachia.
White Grass.
Purchase car top tent/kayak/vest/ski boots/snowboard boots.
Figure out how to carry Bryce's spirit with me everywhere – communicating on an interactive level as "one."

Personal Bucket List 2025

Get understanding. Get peace. Get/re-gain Trust.
Unclutter my mind.
Make my mind strong/take control.
Don't react/be so grounded that I am unshakeable.
Find/heal enough to feel safe – gentleness/humor/trust/kindness
a place/person to give to . . . on the path to discover what true
love actually means.
Continue enjoying my "wardrobe exploration."

BRB/MAMA Bucket List 2025

Canandaigua Lake
Colorado
Overlanding – Andes Mountains
               Swiss Alps/Switzerland
Switzer Lake
Reddish Knob
Montana
Utah – Salt Flats
Splinters – Warren, VT
Ray's Indoor Bike Park
Moab - Utah – to ride bikes
Ice skating

Entity Bucket List

Keep a work/life balance.
Share my knowledge.
Build a support team.

Faith Bucket List

Trust/trust again – enough to communicate and sink
into the Truth.
Re-open – cultivate the conversations/connections with Jesus so
that it is my consistent grounding and foundation.

Bryce's soul IS ALIVE.
Bryce's spirit is with me at all times.
Bryce hears me.
I WILL see Bryce again.
Bryce is teaching me how to live.
God is real.
God is Truth.
God is in control.
God is protecting Bryce.
God has a plan for Bryce.
God has a plan for me.
God will reunite Bryce and me.
I will know LOVE.

Commitment to myself – I take my mind captive – only the thoughts that are healing/uplifting/have grace – are ones I will think about. From this point forward no one has real estate in my mind. No one has a say/authority over me – what others say does not matter. I. AM. ME. I am not waiting for approval or permission from anyone. I will forge my own path with Bryce's spirit at my side.

I declare this year – and those that follow, to be when I rise up – I will NOT fail. I will use the moments given to me – to live, to give, to be transformative.

The Nonprofit

Following the weekend in West Virginia, the looking forward to the next gathering, which was just two weeks away, is what kept me together. For months, the core group had discussed establishing a nonprofit in Bryce's honor. Each of us carries a part of Bryce with us. We bear witness to how Bryce lived. Our goal was to establish a nonprofit to share Bryce's legacy with others – to help others learn to live like Bryce. Our tag line has always been, "What would Bryce do?"

In preparation, I rented a beautiful Airbnb near Massanutten, ordered food for the group, developed the agenda for the nonprofit's brainstorming session and prepared special gifts for those in attendance.

Following a dinner of chicken pot pies made by Greenbarn Bakery in Locust Grove, Virginia (an amazing baker), we began the Brainstorming Session. The Brainstorming Session was attended by the core group, and it was a dynamic sharing of how to continue Bryce's legacy.

The following is the Agenda of the Brainstorming Session.

ELEMENTS OF HOW BRYCE LIVED

SELECTON OF ENTITY TYPE

Foundation: Primarily provides funds to other organizations. Accountable to the IRS

Nonprofit: A charitable organization with a specific goal or mission. Free of restrictions on spending. Accountable to donors and sponsors. Decision making includes choices about which programs to offer, how to allocate resources, and how to measure success. (Nonprofit corporation vs. Nonprofit LLC)

TAX STATUS

501(c)(3): Must be tax-exempt to qualify. Categories: Charitable. Educational. Fostering of national amateur sports.

SETUP

File with the State Corporation Commission (SCC)
Article of Incorporation
Obtain EIN
Apply for tax-exempt status.
Establish by-laws (if a corporation).
Board of Directors Meeting (if a corporation)
  Initial Directors
  President
  Vice President
  Secretary
  Treasurer
  Registered Agent
  Principal Place of Doing Business
Register as a Virginia Charity – Charitable Solicitation.
Conflict of Interest Policy.
Establish a bank account.

File Annual Report.

VISION/PURPOSE

What is the problem/void?
How can we solve it/fill it?

SHORT-TERM GOALS

LONG-TERM GOALS

MISSION STATEMENT

NAME OF ENTITY

Include BRB and reference to "the mission."

BRANDING/LOGO/MARKETING –
"GETTING THE MESSAGE OUT"

FINANCING/BACKING

Seed Money
Storage Space
Donations
Fundraising
Membership Programs

GEOGRAPHICAL SERVICE AREA(S)

INSURANCE

The Brainstorming Session began with me giving each person a copy of the Care and Counsel Bible. For a year, I had wanted to give a copy to each member of the core group. That evening was perfect timing. As you now know, gift giving is one of my love languages – as it was Bryce's. Bryce's accident has rocked my world, and still, as I struggle to regain my footing – even in asking/screaming the "WHY" within the terms of my faith, the

Bible was the most special gift I could think of to give. It was Bryce's favorite Bible, and is buried with his body (if one only knew the tears that flow and the pain that is felt when writing this). The Bibles arrived at 8:30 the night before I headed over the mountain for the Brainstorming Session – perfect timing. Bryce bore witness to his faith to this group – this is one of my ways of continuing his witness.

After presenting the Bibles, I shared some thoughts with the group that were gleaned from *The Fellowship of the Unashamed*, which is an incredible statement on how to live life. In addition to the statement being one that Bryce loved, it is my belief that an entity established in Bryce's honor should have a tenet of faith as an element of its foundation.

The encouragements that were Bryce's takeaways from *The Fellowship of the Unashamed* were deep and guiding truths: to be well-grounded in what matters in life and to truly live that as an example, to give without reservation, to dream big – unconstrained by fear/doubt/provision – and not be hindered by what the world thinks, and to know that at the end of his time on this earth he would be welcomed into Heaven.

Those beliefs – those creeds by which Bryce lived, were the perfect segue into sharing words that describe Bryce.

The following are the NOTES from the Brainstorming Session.

THE BRECKENRIDGE NOMADICS PROJECT
"What would Bryce do?"

Brainstorming Session
January 10th, 2025

NOTES

WORDS THAT DESCRIBE BRYCE

Principled, Full Send, Humble, Selfless, Non-biased, Direct, Faithful, Grounded, Non-distracted – Committed, Integrity, Honest, All-encompassing, Spontaneous, Visionary, Centered

NAME OF ENTITY

THE BRECKENRIDGE NOMADICS PROJECT and the tag line that appears right under the entity's title: "What would Bryce do?"

THE BRECKENRIDGE NOMADICS PROJECT
"What would Bryce do?"

THE BRECKENRIDGE NOMADICS PROJECT – a Nonstock Corporation in the Commonwealth of Virginia; established January 16, 2025.

Katherine owns BRECKENRIDGE NOMADICS, LLC. The entities will support each other (for example, the LLC will sell specific merchandise letting the buyer know the proceeds go to the nonprofit). Think of it as akin to having "sister stores," but one can't make money . . . but the one which makes money can give it to the other (the nonprofit) and direct people in that direction.

MISSION STATEMENT

What would Bryce do? He embodied the FULL SEND effect. Our mission is to teach others how to live like Bryce through the fostering of the national amateur sport of mountain biking, educational forums such as seminars and events, the building and maintenance of mountain bike trails, the loaning of mountain bikes to those who cannot afford them, and the provision of funds to mountain bike programs as well as those injured in the sport. By education, example, and giving, we will foster a FULL SEND lifestyle in others so that they are comfortable going out of their comfort zone; that they will know what it is like to be fully present/fully committed so they can experience moments of all-encompassing freedom.

PRESENT AT THE BRAINSTORMING SESSION

Kolten Windsor, Cody Gray, Luke Martin, Baylor Robinson, Maddie Gray, Jake Fulk, and Katherine Breckenridge

BOARD MEMBERS

Kolten Windsor, Cody Gray, Luke Martin, Baylor Robinson, Maddie Gray, Jenna Gabb, Knox Ryan, and Katherine Breckenridge

DIRECTORS

President: Kolten Windsor
Vice President: Luke Martin
Treasurer: Cody Gray
Secretary: Baylor Robinson

All are in agreement that every member carries the "same weight/influence" whether one has a title or not. Need a non-disclosure agreement.

LOGO

BRECKENRIDGE NOMADICS, LLC, uses and owns the "penciled" image of Bryce mountain biking. The nonprofit will be using the same image with a variation of background/wording.

There will be a written statement/agreement between the two entities about the ownership/use of the logo and a clear mission.

ENTITY

The entity will be a nonprofit as opposed to a foundation.

FOCUS OF THE ENTITY

To teach others to live like Bryce. Begin with mountain biking and at some point, incorporate snowboarding.

> Youth engagement.
> Affordable for those who can't afford it – make it accessible and inspiring (so they love it).
> Build trails – free ride.
> Give money.
> Injury/Accident Fund.

CATEGORIES

> Trails – Volunteers
> Funds
>> For equipment (bikes) to loan.
>> For equipment to build trails.
>> For money to give.
> Educational – How to ride. How to maintain bikes.
> Safety/limits.
>> In schools.
>> Seminars.
>> Events.

Race Team.

Equipment.
> Bikes, Bike maintenance, Trail building.

LONG-TERM GOALS

> Geographical "Service" Area: (1) Harrisonburg,
> (2) Massanutten, (3) Bryce Resort, (4) Shenandoah,
> (5) Virginia, (6) West Virginia, (7) Nationally

> Own land – a facility . . . a hub that includes camping.
> (@10,000 acres)

NEXT MEETING

Friday, February 21st at 5:00 PM, Location TBA. AGENDA for Friday, February 21st

    (1) Plan for April 19th event – The Jam. (Location – Cody's house.)
        a. Needs a waiver.
    (2) April 20th – Soft launch of the nonprofit. – Media
    (3) Hard Launch – Bryce Day
    (4) Funds
    (5) Marketing/Branding

FOLLOWING MEETING

Saturday, March 15th at 5:00 PM, Location TBA.

On the Mountain

The following day, the group went snowboarding/skiing together at Massanutten. The mountain was busy, and parking was hard to find.

Everyone had their gear, except me. I had never snowboarded or skied. Two years ago, Bryce had given me a pair of skis, and it was on my bucket list to ski. I had skis and poles, but no boots or a helmet. The patience of the group was incredible. They made sure I rented boots, and Baylor lent a helmet to me. I did  not have the confidence to get off the lift on skis, let alone try the bunny slope. The group, all of whom were experts, were incredibly patient and accompanied me to the "teaching / learning / assistance area," where Baylor provided me with tips on maintaining my balance while skiing. While Baylor was helping me, the rays of the sun came over the mountain. Cody captured in a photo my FULL SEND sign to Bryce. Bryce was definitely present.

My counselor has told me to watch for small miracles. There was a man about Bryce's age who was just finishing a ski lesson and agreed to give me a lesson. I did not have an appointment, and the timing was perfect. The rest of the group was able to leave me in good hands and finally hit the slopes with their snowboards. In addition to being an incredible instructor (he helped me conquer some fears, and I did not fall once), he also knew Bryce.

He shared with me that he had mountain biked with Bryce and that Bryce was the best mountain biker with whom he had ever ridden. This mama's heart will forever treasure that.

Establishment of the Entity

Upon returning home, I established the entity, THE BRECKENRIDGE NOMADICS PROJECT, with the State Corporation Commission (SCC) on the sixteenth day of January, 2025. When doing so, the names of those on the Board of Directors needed to be submitted.

I was so happy to share with the core group that the dream we had was actually taking root. Half an hour after the establishment of the entity, I received a lengthy text from one in the group sharing that he needs to focus on his career goals and though happy to help with events held by the entity, is unable to dedicate the time needed towards the entity. As much as I understand, support such a decision, celebrate this person's dreams and adventures – as I know Bryce is celebrating them – my heart still ached, as this person is so special to me (and Bryce) and I wanted this person involved as we meet as a group to continue Bryce's legacy.

With the agreement of others in the group, I reached out to Baylor to see if he would take on the Officer position of Secretary. Baylor said yes, and the immediate confirmations from the group were both beautiful and humorous. Jenna's (Baylor's girlfriend) confirmation solicited humor from Kolten, "You sure about that?!" The exchange made me ask Baylor in the same group text chain, "Baylor – You've gotta be feeling the love!!!!" His response, "Ohhhh yea definitely feelin the love!"

BYLAWS

Following the establishment of THE BRECKENRIDGE NOMADICS PROJECT, I spent almost two days drafting the bylaws. Bylaws for a nonprofit need to include many different aspects than a for-profit corporation. To me, these bylaws were like writing a labor of love – they reflect the heart and soul of the goals of the entity.

AGREEMENT OF USE

It is the mutual intent of Katherine S. Breckenridge, BRECKENRIDGE NOMADICS, LLC, and THE BRECKENRIDGE NOMADICS PROJECT, INC., to share with the community (near and far) the full send lifestyle of Bryce Ray Breckenridge. I own a stenciled image of Bryce riding his mountain bike. Since the entities and I have the same intent regarding the sharing of Bryce's full send lifestyle, I wrote a waiver, which licenses the use of the image to THE BRECKENRIDGE NOMADICS PROJECT, reserving the right to withdraw that right due to how much the image means to me.

AGENDA

What helps hold me together are the interactions I have with the core group. Spending a Sunday afternoon preparing the agenda for the next meeting fills in the time between the tears. In addition to the "standard" items included in an agenda when an entity meeting occurs (for example, the review and approval of the minutes from the prior meeting), the following are the highlights set forth for discussion.

MARKETING/BRANDING
Social Media
Documentary
Product/Handouts

THE JAM – April 19th Event
Review and Approval of the Release and Waiver of Liability
Planning
Audience
Advertisement – Getting the word out
Prepping the location
Safety

Entertainment
Food
Handouts
Sponsors

SOFT LAUNCH – April 20th
Social Media

HARD LAUNCH – BRYCE DAY – August 2025

FUNDING

Contributions
Memberships

The three-ring binders for the meeting are prepared and filled with copies of the originating documents, tax forms, and all documents to date. As I have shared, what brings me the greatest pleasure is the giving of gifts. This time I have gift bags filled with mountain biking socks, collapsible camping mugs, Puffin drink covers that look like miniature winter coats, and bookmarks with an inspirational saying about advice from a mountain.

My ski gear is packed. The anticipation builds as we meet the group on Friday evening for pizza, snacks, and great company, followed by a Saturday morning meeting at Thunderbird Café. Then . . . snowboarding at Massanutten Saturday afternoon.

Monday's Phone Call

Forever, I will treasure Cody's phone call. His initial voicemail said, "Mama." That was what Bryce called me. When Cody and I spoke, he shared that knowing Bryce was a privilege. That resonates deeply in my heart, and on which I have reflected since the phone call. As Bryce's mama, I knew how special Bryce was. I remain perplexed and yes, angry regarding those who did not make the time to get to know Bryce, to listen to his wisdom, to trust his insight and perspective, and to truly celebrate the very unique and special man God created. Bryce was a gift to this raw and challenging earth. His soul was perfect.

Advice From Bryce – by KSB

S low down. Nothing is worth getting rattled by a schedule.

Adventure/Explore. Life is too short to live within a comfort zone.

Get up early to watch the sunrise. Sleep is overrated.

Go to the top of the mountain as the sun is setting. A true place to worship.

FaceTime your mama. You are her heart.

Watch the rock designs. That may just be the perfect line.

Ride fast. Don't leave anything on the trail.

Encourage from the sidelines.
Being the center of attention
is for the weak.

Be principled. Do
not waver in your
stance.

Find work that is art
to you. Work hard.

Designs with dirt,
rocks, and wood are
art. Forms with
God's creations.

Say Grace. This is
not by chance.

Respect others. Unless they disrespect you –
No matter the position, rank, or age.

Protect the child.
Be his voice when abuse is present.

Don't judge. Be a better person –
the world needs uniqueness.

Maintain your focus.
Keep your Bible close.

FULL SEND.

Another Mountain Weekend

BREAKFAST WITH THE GROUP

Thunderbird Café was where the group met for an amazing breakfast – stories and pictures of Bryce laced through our conversation.

SECOND SKI LESSON

When I saw that every parking spot was filled and that the line for rentals extended around the rental shop, I should have waived my reserved private lesson.

With the gift of the skis Bryce had given to me, my new helmet, and ski boots – I was determined to have an hour on the slopes (though I was on the "I Need Assistance Slope") – closer to Bryce.

I had a wonderful instructor – she shared her expertise and allowed me to speak about Bryce – to show her pictures. She extended my lesson due to the ski fittings that needed to occur. This time I learned the meaning of "pizza!" Now, I could stop. Halfway through the lesson another "newbie" had not learned how to "pizza" and ran into me full-force while my back was turned. Even as others had to help me get up, I knew right away that I was hurt and that recovery was going to take some time. Though nothing was broken, eight weeks later, my shoulder has not recovered.

Though the accident shook me, in full Bryce fashion, that "bruise" is not going to deter me, and next year – I will return . . . likely to the "I Need Assistance Slope."

THE STEEL WHEELS

Bryce introduced me to a music genre that has been a lifeline for me. I have tried to have a "concert attendance" or "festival attendance" on my calendar – giving me something to look forward to.

That evening, Baylor, Jenna, their friends, and I attended a concert by The Steel Wheels. It was a full house and our seats were in the balcony.

The show was AMAZING! So many of their songs spoke to me. The lyrics of Ready, "No longer building a tower. Gave up on wearing a crown." - so profound, and it was how Bryce lived.

The "spirit of performance," which I have wrestled with all of my life, is fading and taking a backseat. Having always sought the leadership role – now all I want is Bryce back. All I want is to be wherever Bryce is.

RETURNING TO HOME

The return home again hit like a ton of bricks. The tears flowed for two days – it was like walking in a daze. I had given everything I had and then some for the weekend's plans, and Bryce still was not here. The pain was too great.

Music

I have referenced my introduction by Bryce to a very special music genre. The following are a few of the bands and music selections that have helped hold me. The lyrics may not sound like worship or praise songs; however, they resonate in this mama's heart, inspiring a deep reflection of faith for me.

Three I have already mentioned:

- *Feathered Indians* (and *Follow You to Virgie* and *Sour Mash*) by Tyler Childers
- *The Very Best*
  Sung by Buffalo Wabs & The Price Hill Hustle
- *Ready* by The Steel Wheels

From that base, I kept searching and the gems keep surfacing, to include:

- *Ghost of My Best Friend* by Arlo McKinley (I hold on tightly to this one.)
- *Wide River to Cross* by the White Horse Guitar Group
- Sierra Ferrell's singing of *Don't Let Me Down* (by the Beatles)
- *By the Way* and *Ships in the Harbor* by Tommy Prine
- *Wasting Time* (and *S.O.B.)* by Nathaniel Rateliff & The Night Sweats
- *Summer's End* by John Prine
- *Rethink Clean* by Jesse Welles
- *Time's All I Got* by Matt Mason

Bryce and I loved our record player – there is something magical about listening to the above via vinyl.

The Breckenridge Nomadics Project
Meeting Minutes

Friday, February 21, 2025
Location: Rockingham County, Virginia
Time: 5:00 PM

WELCOME

Sharing of Bryce's message (writer is The Wandering Paddy on Instagram) – "Tell the stories that made me live. . . . Remember the times we swore we'd never forget . . . and don't. I was here, a life well lived. So raise a glass and dance a little. Let the wind take my name . . . I'll be listening. Do not mourn me, celebrate me."

PRESENT AT THE MEETING

Kolten Windsor, Luke Martin, Cody Gray, Baylor Robinson, Jenna Gabb, Madeline Gray, and Katherine Breckenridge

BYLAWS/NOTICE OF ELECTION OF OFFICERS/AGREEMENT OF USE

Review and discussion of the draft Bylaws, Notice of Election of Officers, and Agreement of Use Acceptance by a Unanimous Vote and Execution of Bylaws, Notice of Election of Officers, and Agreement of Use

Next step(s) - Application with the IRS for nonprofit status

APPROVAL OF MINUTES

Discussion of and Unanimous Approval of the Minutes of the Meeting of the Board on January 10, 2025

MARKETING/BRANDING

Social-Media: Luke will initiate and design accounts with Facebook, Instagram, and maybe TikTok – with each Board

Member having sign in authority. Jake's video will be used as a "base" with additional images and text added.

Kolten will establish the entity's email:
FULLSEND@BRECKENRIDGENOMADICSPROJECT. COM

Product/Handouts
Kolten and Cody will present "product/handout" options using "The Bryce Image." The options will include type/number (price break level)/and cost(s).

Documentary
Jenna is going to reach out to her brother regarding capturing images of our efforts – both at The Jam and perhaps ongoing. Luke is going to reach out to his contact regarding compiling a documentary.

THE JAM – April 19th Event
Reviewed and unanimous approval of the Release and Waiver of Liability
Planning
Audience – Design "golden ticket" and wristbands – KSB
At the next meeting, have a list of the participants each Board Member will invite.
Advertisement – Getting the word out

Prepping the location
The dirt is coming. 4 – 6 loads needed. Jenna's friend may be able to get dirt. Cody has a contact/supplier and machinery. By the meeting on March 15th, Cody will let us know how much dirt he can get and when it is going to be delivered. By the meeting on March 15th, Cody, Kolten, Luke, and Baylor will confirm the "lines" (the mapping) to be developed/finished (i.e. kids' line, big line, medium line – with the trails coming to the bottom left corner)

Bathroom Facilities
(As well as an overnight option for a place to stay.)
Maddie is going to check with the two adjacent Airbnb rentals.

Safety
Cody will announce the rules.
Jake/Luke/Maddie – all "certified"
Post signs – "Ride at your own risk."
Waiver for riders (approved by the Board)
Include a Waiver for signature by a Parent/Guardian – KSB
Draft Waiver for Spectator – KSB
"Use Agreement" between the entity and the landowners

Entertainment
Luke and Cody both know bands and will reach out to them. We
need to know what the bands need in order to perform.
Consider hiding action figures.

PRIZES
Adult Rider Competition – Award
Kids' Competition - Award
The Bryce Award (Adults)
    – Best all-around character/energy
The Jr. Bryce Award (Children)
    – Best all-around character/energy

Food
Pizza, hot dogs (maybe deer burgers), chili, soda, water

Handouts
See above under "Products/Handouts" (shirts/OG Reserve,
stickers, hats, bandanas – maybe OG Reserve burned into wood)

Sponsors
First Choice HVAC
Jenna's brother's company

AGENDA FOR NEXT MEETING –
SATURDAY, MARCH 15th at 5:00 PM, Place TBD

NONPROFIT APPLICATION STATUS

THE JAM – Saturday, April 19th – Location the Gray's House
> Update on schedule and all planning items.

SOFT LAUNCH – April 20th
Social Media

HARD LAUNCH – BRYCE DAY – August 2025

FUNDING
Contributions
Memberships

WEBSITE
DONATIONS
SPONSORSHIPS
MEMBERSHIPS
PODCASTS

This week, I focused on the items I had committed to address during the last meeting. I removed Jake's name from the Directors with the State Corporation Commission (SCC) and included Knox's name as a Director. I filed for nonprofit status with the IRS. I filed the Business Ownership Interests (BOI) with FinCEN (Financial Crimes Enforcement Network). I wrote the Lease of Land for The Jam, Parent/Guardian Waiver for The Jam, and the Spectator Waiver for The Jam.

More Hurtful Comments

"Some may say you have overdone it. That is their right to view however they wish." WAIT, WHAT?!????!!! Let me rephrase . . . WTF?!?!?!?! NO ONE should EVER sit in judgment of a mama who has lost her child!!!! Am I not grieving in a manner that is acceptable to you?!!! Well, leave my world then. And, to say, "It is their right to view however they wish." NO IT IS NOT!!! They have no clue – no right whatsoever.

"If you have truly accepted Christ as Lord and Savior, you will see Bryce again." DON'T EVER say that to a grieving mama!!! The "If you have truly" sounds like judgment to me. How in the world could you make such a statement – especially knowing that my faith is the very fiber of who I am? A rephrase would have been balm for this mama's heart . . . "I know you will see Bryce again when Jesus welcomes you home."

"I miss our everyday sharing and laughing." When reading that, I hear the following: I've not performed just right. I'm not enough. I've disappointed. Well, yes - I f***ing miss "the Katherine before the accident," too. I miss "that Katherine" more than anyone!" Grief is like a weighted fog that permeates the mind and body. It is hard work to just exist.

"I know you are full of sorrow. But I'm praying you will reflect the love of God in the midst of sorrow and choose to reflect joy based on Truth of Him being sovereign." I am trying my best to survive . . . WHY is it important that I am pouring out to others during this time? The comment felt like such a performance-based statement. What human created that falsity!?! Isn't that the box from which I am trying to break free?

"It's just things." REALLY?!?!!!! Maybe things are "just things" in a divorce, but CERTAINLY NOT in regards to the accident. I wouldn't give away a sock!!!! What I have is finite – it is ALL I HAVE LEFT OF BRYCE!

"I hope it was a graduation." Again, WTF!?!!! WHY would you say that to a grieving mama? What if I wasn't sure of Bryce's eternity? How egregious would such a statement be? Thankfully, I trust that Bryce is a place that is so incredibly wonderful that a human brain cannot conceptualize such beauty.

Reflecting on her own family, a statement made matter-of-factly and confidently about her personal family: "We don't expect our children to die before us." Wait? What? You are blatantly making that statement in front of a mama whose son is no longer on this earth. Are you kidding me?

"Do your clients mind your phone message?"

"I promise you that in time you will miss your son the same way you miss an aunt or uncle." Again, WTF?!?!!?!!!!!!

Voice mail left in response to my request for some grace as I come to terms with my son's passing . . . "WOW, that certainly is inconvenient." And, again, WTF?!?!!!!!!

Trying to Make a Birthday Happy

What to do with a birthday day!?! WHY do I get to see fifty-nine years, and my precious son did not get to see twenty-seven years? The thread to which I grasp is that I am now one day closer to being with Bryce.

The sorrow is so deep – an invasive permanence, but I keep on waking up and trying, trying, trying to keep going. If it wasn't for my daughter and Lincoln, I would not remain here. That is hard for some to hear, but it is the truth.

We celebrated a day early. My daughter and parents made the day special. Wanting to share a memorable birthday meal with my parents – Clare, Tommy (Clare's boyfriend), and I went in search of the world's best crabcakes . . . Talk of the Mountain Crabcakes. The hour-long wait for the food to be ready was worth it. We shared an incredible meal with my parents following their seven-hour drive. And, birthday dessert was an amazing strawberry-chocolate cake from Greenbarn Bakery.

Though the food provided comfort, it was the sharing that communicated, "I see you, I know you," that touched this mama's heart. Clare gave me a card that stated, "Mountain Warrior" – the outside picture looks like Lincoln and me hiking and the inside is a statement of both Clare and Bryce's love. And, the newest sticker for my banjo case . . . "Mountain Mama" already decorates the silver beauty!

Today, the actual "day of aging" – is spent weeping . . . trying to love Bryce back onto this earth.

Special moments – Starbucks and a hug from Clare, saying "good-bye" to my parents as they continue on their travels, a walk in the park listening to Bryce's and my favorite song,

"Feathered Indians," and then three occurrences that deeply touched my heart.

The first . . . The core group sent me a dozen roses and the note said, "From Bryce and the Core Group." This precious group of friends reached into my day when I was a ball of tears - missing precious Bryce so so so much!!! Their love, friendship and actions in keeping Bryce's love and legacy alive speak to how special they

are. They are amazing and each carries a part of Bryce with them, and I celebrate that!

The second occurrence . . . Today, the sail made it home. I wish I could put into words how much this means. It was the sail I used as a child and the sail Bryce used. When my parents sold my grandparent's cottage on the lake, parting with the small sailboat, the Phantom, broke Bryce's heart. For years, Bryce said the one thing he would like

returned to him was this sail. Today, it is home. And, I cannot stop crying. I lay on the sail in the middle of the yard – wept and spoke with Bryce.

The third occurrence . . . Cody's phone call. Bryce loved Cody, and on this day that should be one spent with Bryce . . . Cody "stands in the gap." Bryce would have loved this. I know Bryce knows.

Stretch Marks

That day, as I stood in the office bathroom to wash my hands, I glanced at the mirror while tucking in my shirt and noticed my stretch marks.

The wave of understanding that the stretchmarks were caused by Bryce created moments of absolute joy. It hit me that they are beautiful – they are proof that Bryce was present – that he was once a baby growing inside of me. NEVER, EVER will I see my stretchmarks as anything but wonderful – they seemed akin to the body's natural correlation of a tattoo. I wanted to shout my excitement to anyone who would listen – I did not. Not many would understand. To those who do understand – don't try to hide the proof of existence . . . celebrate those stretchmarks.

Anger Beneath the Surface

I remember taking a walk with an Assistant Dean while I was in law school. She had recently lost her father. When I asked how she was doing, her reply was, "It is the same in death as it was in life." How true that now seems. Lyrics in The Steel Wheels' song "*Heaven Don't Come by Here*," bear testimony to that truth.

"Don't bring your flowers
Nothing here grows
Don't bring your flowers
Like you didn't know
Don't bring your flowers anymore, anymore, anymore"

Bryce and I protected each other and had reason to do so. In his death, this mama bear's love and protection continues. If you didn't love and care for precious Bryce during life – if you didn't give him time, show up for him, respect who he was, listen to his dreams, truly and deeply care for him in a manner that Bryce trusted and received – keep your tokens.

Searching for Answers

**Wrestling with a theologian's words.
Proof of Bryce's Eternal Existence**

Artwork by Knox

I have said it before, and I will say it again, there is not enough oxygen in the world to provide sufficient breath to a mama who has lost a child. I. Miss. Bryce. To. My. Core. I don't like life. I am going through the motions of living. There seems to be no purpose left. If I had known how painful this journey was, I would have chosen to leave this earth shortly after Bryce's accident. Now, I remain here because I would not wish that pain on my daughter. And, I provide the care and love for Lincoln, the dog Bryce gave to me years prior to the accident.

The pain is horrible, and even when there are no answers, I find incredible comfort in George McDonald's quote, made famous by C.S. Lewis, "A body doesn't have a soul, a soul has a body." Counting that as truth, that would mean that even if Bryce's body did not work because of the accident, his soul is still present – still alive – still flourishing. I will cling to that HOPE.

Shaken to the Core

In C.S. Lewis's book, A Grief Observed, he addressed the grief he experienced at the loss of his wife. This book was unlike any other book I had read by C.S. Lewis. Part of me wishes I had not read it, and I wonder whether he intended for it to be published. Perhaps I wonder that because of the harsh "takeaways" that I personally interpreted from it.

I was so "shaken" by *my* two "takeaways" that I asked to process them with my counselor. They were: (1) Did God allow his wife to die because C.S. Lewis loved his wife more than God? (2) Following his wife's death, did C.S. Lewis hold on to his faith because he knew that was the one, the only means of seeing his wife again?

Whether or not that is someone else's interpretation of what the author was communicating, it was mine, and it left me reeling. It was an uncomfortable consideration, a very personal one for this grieving mama.

Did I love Bryce more than God? Could this whole, horrible cruelty be because I loved Bryce so much? Am I now working my way back to God's Truth because I know that is the only hope I will have to see my precious Bryce again?

I laid these questions at the feet of my counselor. His reply – full of wisdom – was in the form of a question. Is it possible that I love Bryce so much because I see reflections of God in Bryce? WOW!! I drew comfort from the process that ensued – I thought about Bryce's attributes. How was Bryce made in God's image? Bryce was physically beautiful. When one looked into his eyes, it was like looking into a wise, pure, older soul. Bryce was kind. I had observed him on many occasions giving the little money he had to the homeless on the sidewalk benches. Bryce was non-judgmental – even if he did not agree, he argued for another's right to live freely. Bryce never needed to be the center of attention – he was present, he was observant, yet the whole room gravitated around him. Bryce was quiet, yet when he spoke his thoughts were full of wisdom and people listened. Bryce's theological questions were deep, searching, and profound. Bryce's faith was not constrained within bricks and mortar – he worshipped in the wilderness, often at the highest peak. He saw God's wonder in a snowflake, at the rising and setting of the sun, in the rock formations and dirt paths.

Yes, in Bryce, I saw God's love and perfect creation. Before Bryce's accident my constant conversation was with God, so I pushed back against that first question that haunted me from *A Grief Observed*. It is not that I love Bryce more than God, it is that I recognized – as a mama does, a son – beautifully and wonderfully made.

To the second personal observation – that perhaps I am working my way back to the Truth because I know that is my only hope that I will see Bryce again.

I draw reflection upon the following . . . when evil is removed from one's life, there is still a foundation from which to build . . . when the evil was in human form. When joy is removed from one's life – a joy embodied in a human . . . what now?!??? Bryce was joy to me (oh, I know the pushback here – a human can bring happiness, but joy is supernatural and therefore always present and unshakeable) . . . for now, just humor me and allow me to use the interchangeable words of Bryce and JOY. The changing of a soul within the realms is almost too much for the mind, heart, and spirit to comprehend – to wrap one's mind around. Thus, the "building back" – the grasping for a foundation that has been shaken . . . this is hard work.

When I find myself questioning and seemingly on shaky ground, I observe my surroundings and contemplate creation's existence, concluding time and time again that chance did not create this. Therefore, my goal of steadying myself with the Truth is not out of a question as to whether God exists, because to me he conclusively does, it is recognizing that I hurt, my world was shattered, that the trauma I have experienced is unbearable and that though I have been shaken and my heart and mind blurred on the path of life, I need for my very existence/for who I am to the core – and who Bryce is . . . to clear the fog, to be able to again stand steadfast. This does not mean that the pain will lessen, that life will be okay – I have no answers for why the accident occurred, why the one person who truly brought a pure, unencumbered lifestyle to this harsh and raw earth was allowed to be taken, why a mama would ever have to bear this sorrow. What I do know is that no matter how hard the path may be, irrespective of the presented obstacles, I will keep reaching for – living with the Truth . . . Bryce would want that, too.

Finding Comfort

In C.S. Lewis's book, *Letters to Malcom, Chiefly on Prayer*, C.S. Lewis speaks to the disparity or contrast between Heaven and Earth. He talks about our earthly actions and activities as being almost meaningless ways of passing time, as if they are not even a precursor to what Heaven is like. I venture to say the time spent here is but a placeholder. C.S. Lewis references Heaven as being "a complete reconciliation of boundless freedom with order," and that Earth is not a representation of Heaven.

What was one of my favorite quotes prior to Bryce's accident, and to which I now cling in the ultimate hope and belief that Bryce is now eternally experiencing, is, "Dance and game are frivolous, unimportant down here; for 'down here' is not their natural place. Here, they are a moment's rest from the life we were placed here to live. But in this world, everything is upside down. That which, if it could be prolonged here, would be a truancy, is likest that which in a better country is the End of ends. Joy is the serious business of Heaven."

Even as I deeply grieve that Bryce is not here; that I am no longer able to take care of him and provide for him the way this mama loved doing; that my mind wonders if he is cold and has what he needs, and that Bryce will forever by twenty-six years of age … if my precious Bryce is now and will forever more know a perfect joy – an existence that is inconceivable to this mama's shattered heart . . . then I will somehow, though I don't want to, make it through today and possibly the next.

While Here – Clinging to Those Who Embody Parts of Bryce

The core group each holds a different part of Bryce in them. Though this mama clings to them as the interactions bring Bryce closer, losing Bryce is truly closing an irreplaceable window into the world. Bryce saw people, relationships, faith, and actions through eyes and a heart unique unto him. There will never be another Bryce, and as the days progress, this mama is realizing that I cannot love him back onto this earth, that I cannot give gifts or create events that will bring Bryce back, and that when the gatherings are over and when I return home, Bryce will not be here.

The pain of this realization is beyond words – that there is a void in my little world and in the great expanse of life on this earth that will never be filled. C.S. Lewis embodied the emptiness and the now eternal missing link perfectly in his book, *The Four Love Languages.*

I have been able to reflect that "link" in how Bryce interacted with others. When Bryce was here on this earth, those close to him enjoyed how he reacted to and interacted with those around him. Bryce was "the glue;" through his kindness, insightfulness, and humor, he brought out aspects of others – like laughter and deep thinking that otherwise may not have been forthcoming within the group. Bryce truly augmented friendships. Without Bryce here, we are trying to "re-weave" our ties – knowing we won't see each other through Bryce's eyes, but we strive to use the parts of Bryce we carry within each of us so that the braid of deep friendship flourishes.

It is this mama's hope that the void left by Bryce here on this earth will one day be perfected in Heaven.

Conversations at the Feet of Clouds

Early this morning, I wept while viewing the cloud formations. The heart in the sky – the blue of the sky . . . you were listening. I shared how I love being your mama. It is the greatest joy of my life. Now, my life has little to no meaning. I am struggling to find value – in living and in myself. I loved providing for you, listening to you, sharing with you, dreaming of your future with you, sharing about faith, and all the seemingly little things that mama's do for their sons – that right now are priceless to me . . . folding your clothes, buying groceries for you, ordering pizza and French fries, opening the gate when you were just a mile from home, sitting outside as you cleaned out your car and exclaimed over the mechanisms of tools you found buried under clothing; I miss your presence, your voice, your smiled, your laughter, the blue of your eyes and how they looked deep into my soul – how they saw things of meaning.

Pain and Insight From a Sibling

Thoughts and Prayers
By: Clare – Bryce's sister

The headline to the post – insert name – has passed away.
Like vultures the "connections" swarm to post the first comment.
Thoughts and prayers.
Rest in peace.
Heaven gained an angel.
Whew conscience cleared.
No other thoughts given.
Back to scrolling. Ha! This meme is great!
The duty is done. Life goes on.

Thoughts and prayers. Rest in peace. Heaven gained an angel.
That mama stares in disbelief.
How heartless.
How selfish.
My baby got his wings & these are the things they think to post.
My life just changed.
My world just turned.
But your thoughts and prayers absolve you.
Can you turn back time?
At least share a picture?
What about a memory? The one where you guys went fishing?
What about the games you played as children?
Or his college years?
Something?
What prayer was said – do you care to share? Of course not. You just posted those thoughtless words instead.

The world keeps spinning.
Someone's world just left.
Keep your thoughts and prayers.

Yea . . . that would be best.
If you have nothing else to offer – offer them that. There is no
kindness in that comment.
There's no benefit for the grieving.
Don't offer them that.

Offer them a shoulder they can cry on without judgment.
Offer a story so they can keep hearing of their loved one.
Offer to share pictures so they can see their face.
Let them have space to talk because all they want is to say their
name.

Keep your thoughts and prayers.

They're not an absolution. They're meaningless words meant to
clear your conscience.

484 Days

Kolten – the one who held you, stayed by your side during your last breathing moments, having gathered the courage to once again ride his motocross bike – posted the following today.

"484 days since I last touched a bike . . .

Those of you that know, know why.

And man let me tell you the explosion of emotions that was had . . .

Honestly, I didn't know if this day would ever happen for me again, but thanks to some good friends for making that first time back extra special!

Special shoutout to Cody for filming the whole thing, despite me griping about it!

#BRB #WhatWouldBryceDo"

When I saw Kolten's Facebook post, I sat in my car and wept; 484 days was a lifetime, especially when my life was so intertwined with Bryce's life. How had this amount of time passed? The pain was as fresh – if not worse – than the day of the accident.

It took at least thirty minutes before I had the composure to send a message to Kolten. The message to me was that Bryce is remembered and celebrated, and that Bryce means so much to his core group of friends who continue to take action in Bryce's honor, doing so the way Bryce would – holding nothing back.

Kolten followed that by sharing in a text message to me, "I can't lie, I broke down and cried like a baby after my first time out. I was so scared (for multiple reasons) but it felt right, and it also felt like a weight off my chest. It was hard to face my fear and do it, but I knew it was something I had to do. It was a true Full Send moment."

Popcorn

Walking into a room and seeing a bottle of Bryce's popcorn . . . the popcorn he will never pop. – There are no words – what seems so simple is gut-wrenching.

A Cardinal in the Yard

I am a mess today – grief is making everything hurt. The one positive/poignant time was early this morning, when a cardinal showed himself four times while I was outside with Lincoln. He sang beautifully/boldly; I am not sure I have ever heard a cardinal in such form. I know it was Bryce.

A CARDINAL ON THE STREET SIGN

Pulling away from the house – the energy it took to get myself from my bed to the car indescribable . . . Shoving the tears back, touching Bryce's picture as I try to instill courage in myself – I looked up and there was a male cardinal on the street sign in front of my home – the home that Bryce once shared with me. I let the world stop – I set aside the office agenda that awaited. I rolled down the window and for what seemed like at least five minutes, I spoke with Bryce – the cardinal sat and listened . . . "Bryce, you are my world. I love you so much. Do you have what you need? Are you warm? I don't know how I am going to get through even just today. I want to be with you – wherever you are. Are you in a place that is so wonderful that I could never imagine the beauty? If so, I will endure this time here – I can somehow do that as long as you are okay." I wept – and wept.

After a Day

Pulling up to my house . . . the transition is hard. I sit in my car for moments seemingly without end – it is too painful to enter an empty house.

I look at pictures that span twenty-six years . . . I want those moments back – and, I want new moments. Not this. Not this ending too soon. Not this finite/permanent shit. I. WANT. MY. SON. BACK.

My Voice

Where is my voice?! Was I not enough then . . . and, so hard to raise my cry – I was not strong enough to place my boundary walls and my precious children suffered because of that . . . again, am I not enough now and why did my voice/my wish/my prayer/my claim not matter?! – To this – this horrible, permanence.

During this lifetime, my interactions/responses have been about making others comfortable. I have used calm words, words of negotiation, a mediation of sorts – that is what polite society requires, or so I have believed. At what expense? At the expense of whom?

Even now. EVEN NOW – when asked how I am – my reply is tailored to make others comfortable, my smile masking that I am completely broken, that I do not want to remain on this earth, that there is no band-aid or balm for this deep wound. I love Bryce deeply, unreservedly – the level of grief is a mirror of that depth.

When dawn arrives – I get myself to work – it takes everything I have to get this body laden with grief, this mind filled with confusion, this shattered spirit out the door. I come home to a silent house. Though the days are a surreal survival drill, I long for the end of each day – deceived in my thinking, I can close the door on that day and welcome the solitude of night – only to be besieged with a wrestling match in my mind as the darkness looms. There is no moment of peace.

Again, where is my voice? How did another day go by, and I put on my black suit and pearls and did not completely lose my shit? The anger, grief, brokenness – all suppressed within this shell so that the offense of expression does not escape, does not offend . . . If you knew how broken I am, would you say hello?

If you knew how broken I am, would you find the courage to be present? If you knew how broken I am, would you stay?

In the solitude, the chosen isolation, I have no one to call, no one to talk to – the belief of a mama grieving. Alone – so wanting to hear Bryce's voice, "Hey, Mama – How are you doing?"

Holy Week

The sun is setting – a bright ball of orange that lights up the sky as it descends behind the Blue Ridge Mountains – Bryce's mountains. The conversation with Bryce wanders between thoughts . . . Were you at a commemorative banquet table last night with Jesus at the head? Are you amongst Heaven's angels today in remembrance of Christ's body changing realms? What is the "waiting period" like? Is there a beauty that transcends my human imagination of the celebration that Easter Sunday will bring?

When I try to reflect and be reverent of the Truth and amazement of this Holy Week, my mind seems to shut down just shortly into the thoughts, like a wall being erected as a protective response. The enormity of where you are – the time and space that stands between us . . . it is just too much for this mama's heart. As my shattered heart and broken spirit move from minute to minute and room to room – still in a fog . . . I pray – I hope that the beauty and pureness of your being is truly an Easter celebration unlike any other.

I have plastic eggs that go unfilled this year . . . there is no one for whom to design the Easter treasure hunt . . . I have tried to remain calm – to refocus my mind when I physically am prone to double-down at the thought of you not being here, of being so far away that I can't reach you. The darkness of this Friday is looming, emphasizing the vastness of the world and the smallness of my being at the same time, magnifying my pain and extreme aloneness.

As the darkness of Friday transitioned into Saturday and I think of how very finite we are, I remind myself that this life is not by chance. I do not have any answers for why bad things happen to good people, to the very best of people. What I do know is that Bryce went somewhere I can find him. I will see Bryce again – that is what keeps me going; but for that, what would be the point?

For now, I am not sure how to get through this night – a time where I both dread and anticipate tomorrow's arrival. Will the Hope I know to be true, truly feel real between the tears that are already falling as my precious Bryce is not here, and I will spend the day alone – trying to move as if against the current – headlong into a wall of grief.

The blue eyes that smile back at me from his picture, looking deep into my soul . . . "He sorta looks like Jesus," shared my aunt. Tonight, I will cling to that observation. It is hard to put into words the puzzle pieces my mind is trying to arrange as I give credence to that statement. Trusting that Bryce was made in God's Image, is it possible that Heaven looks very different than what we have conceptualized? What does being eternally attached to God – to being made whole – to being pure, look like?

At the turn of this new day, somewhere someone is putting on their Sunday best – for many, it is their Easter best. Putting on my Sunday best has nothing to do with clothing. I cannot gather the courage to enter the front door of bricks-and-mortar, nor listen to a sermon from one who has not walked this road.

I absolutely want to experience the sweet beauty of Jesus . . . I am trying to find that path – my path. I spent the early morning hours in the backyard reading from Bryce's Bible and talking with Bryce. The verse that resonated with me is Luke 24:5-6, "Why do you seek the living among the dead? He is not here, but is risen!" Perhaps that is it. Though this human feeling – the one called "missing Bryce" is breaking me, if/when I can pivot in my mind and heart with the Truth – to completely trust that Bryce is amongst the living . . . the REALLY LIVING – for an eternity and in such a beautiful, pure existence, then I can bear this time-period. God has given us a way to get to Him and in doing so has given me a way to get to Bryce.

As the hours pass throughout this day and the days ahead, I so long to know, to really know, the connection between Resurrection, Hope, Truth, and Trust. May those concepts merge and be one in the same in my heart – to affect such will for me mean more than survival in my days left on this earth. Could it mean a pivot in time where I might, just might be able to celebrate that Bryce wasn't robbed of anything, in fact, that he was given the greatest advance?

Halfway through this holy day, I have tried to put "positive" in front of me – to focus on its deep significance. I even put together an Easter egg hunt for Lincoln, the dog Bryce gave to me. Then the broken me took over, and in my isolation, I wept and rocked myself as if a mere child. Bryce was PURE and GOOD and FULL OF LIFE . . . Why, why why????? Grief is not kind.

To Live Fully

Bryce showed me how to live.

Bryce walked a straight line – his way, principled/kind/forthright/insightful – he knew what is important in life – most of us, including me . . . blind until now.

He was never caught up in judgment, in small thinking, in the expectations of others . . . he dreamed big – without boundaries. He was adventurous. He found beauty where it is unsurpassable – not in manmade items, but in the forest, in the sky, and in the water.

Isolation and Then Discovery

I would rather be in isolation than be in a group of people. I want to say Bryce's name – freely without restraint. In a group, it seems the conversations focus on everything BUT. Unless one has experienced this indescribable pain, one cannot comprehend how challenging it is to exist, to continue to converse, or to even leave the house.

SOLO CAMPING:
RED WING ROOTS MUSIC FESTIVAL

Red Wing Roots touched my life deeply. Bryce had introduced me to the music genre played at Red Wing. Red Wing was held at the Natural Chimneys in Mt. Solon, Virginia. It is the artistic creation/genius of The Steel Wheels.

None of Bryce's friends were able to join me for the four-night camping trip, and I was determined to still attend. Supplied with my tent, canopy, Blackstone, and plenty of food to share with those in other campsites, I made the trek alone and entered a magical oasis.

I did it . . . and felt like a bit of a badass! This was my first solo-camping trip – it was beautiful, poignant, and perfect. In addition to experiencing incredible music with Bryce's spirit alongside me – moving alone and as my heart prompted between music stages (meeting wonderful people in the transitions – others who had lost a child, faced a challenge, and who leant an ear and opened their hearts), I had the most amazing massage, found wonderful food, sat in the river, and met new now life-long friends (Steve, Jennifer, Tim, and David . . . It's time for breakfast!)!!!

My heart, which is so raw as I struggle to come to terms with such loss – a place where there is not enough oxygen, felt moments of happiness at Red Wing. In addition to hearing new music groups, standing alongside a large group of people as we collectively joined The Steel Wheels singing, "*Red Wing*" –

"*When my time has come, and all my days are done. If heaven waits, we'll breach the gates. On her wings we'll be one . . .*" by Trent Wagler – as tears streamed down this mama's cheeks, my heart felt connections – a knowing that I am not alone.

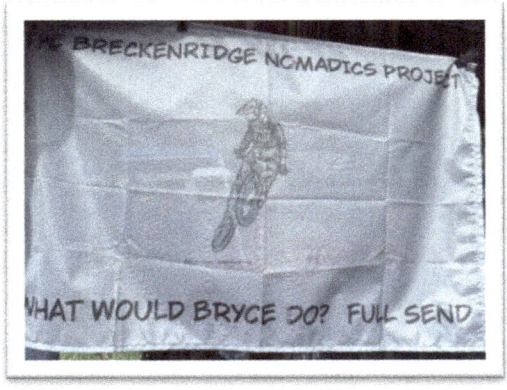

As I departed Monday morning – pulling away (and, so wanting to hold on to the moments of the weekend), I felt such gratitude for the music, the talent, the planning, the expertise, the willingness of those who shared, the setting, the incredible dedication and effort, the vision, and the many kindnesses of the team and volunteers. They touched this mama's heart and the lives of so many! The gift given is priceless. I so look forward to Red Wing Roots XIII.

Summer's Arrival

How is that you were not here during this Winter – your favorite season – and Spring has passed and Summer has arrived? There is such new growth, and you are not here? You would now be on a daily adventure – mountain biking somewhere beautiful.

How is it possible that nineteen months have passed since you walked this earth? How will I make it another day? I see the color of your eyes in the sky – that blue that was unique to only you, and I know you are present. I may not be able to see you in your beautiful, physical form, but even when my heart is breaking and I cannot breathe, and the pain of missing you is a searing, indescribable feeling, I know you are present.

Moving through each moment takes an extraordinary amount of energy. I still scream every day. I weep when I am not in client meetings. Nighttime is horrible – the universe is so big, so daunting now that you are not physically here.

The world thinks a grieving mama should still be able to function – certainly since some time has passed. In my heart, I understand something few do (nor do I ever want them to be in such a position) – there is truly not much into which we invest our time, energy, and worries that really matters. The mundane, the politics, the pontificating, the judgment, the fancy objects, the reserves of resources . . . all pale in comparison to what life really means – how time, that one person, that love shared, is worth everything – is priceless and incomparable.

If God allows me to see daylight tomorrow, my mind will once again – as it does every. single. day. reprocess that my precious son – my person – is not on earth, that I will not hear his voice, that I cannot hug him, that I will not be able to see his beautiful blue eyes . . . the tears will fall, I will again gasp for air, my mind will try to recalibrate the recognition of this nightmare . . . I will literally force myself out of bed against the "gazillion" pound weight of grief.

I may appear to be functioning in my black suit and pearls, but I am not; I am breaking inside. I can work because that is the "structure" I have always known . . . that is not living.

Bryce – I will say your name all day – out loud and in my heart.
I will speak of you to all who will listen. Please, please listen.

I will keep trying to find beauty – trying to live . . . I am doing
that for you, my precious Bryce. What I do know is that each
day brings me closer to you.

We'll meet again on the mountain.

FULL SEND!

Permissions

Chip Chase/ Owner: *White Grass Touring Center*
Whitegrass.com

The Wandering Paddy / James Mooney, 2025.
The Book of Truths
Black & White Publishing

The Steel Wheels
Trenton Andrew Wagler (BMI)/Old Songs Publishing (BMI)
Heaven Don't Come by Here
Ready
Red Wing

Willy Tea Taylor
The Very Best

Sara Groves
Tent in the Center of Town
What Do I Know
All Rights Reserved. Used By Permission.
Copyright: © 1999 Sara Groves Music (Administered by
Music Services) All Rights Reserved. ASCAP

Letters to Malcolm: Chiefly on Prayer
by C.S. Lewis
Copyright © 1963, 1964 C.S. Lewis Pte. Ltd.
Extract reprinted by permission.

www.ingramcontent.com/pod-product-compliance
Lightning Source LLC
Chambersburg PA
CBHW051518120626
46551CB00012B/978